# Tudor Rebellions

FOURTH EDITION

## ANTHONY FLETCHER AND DIARMAID MacCULLOCH

Maps by Leo Vernon

LONGMAN
LONDON

Addison Wesley Longman Limited
Edinburgh Gate,
Harlow, Essex CM20 2JE,
United Kingdom
*and Associated Companies throughout the world*

*Published in the United States of America
by Addison Wesley Longman Inc., New York*

First published 1968
Second edition 1973
Third edition 1983
Fourth edition 1997

ISBN 0 582 28990 4

**British Library Cataloguing in Publication Data**

A catalogue record for this book is available from the British Library

**Library of Congress Cataloging-in-Publication Data**

Fletcher, Anthony.
Tudor rebellions / Anthony Fletcher and Diarmaid MacCulloch. --
4th ed.
         p. cm.
   Includes bibliographical references and index.
   ISBN 0-582-28990-4
   1. Great Britain--History--Tudors, 1485–1603. 2. Peasant uprisings--Great
Britain--History--16th century. 3. Insurgency--Great Britain--History--16th century.
I. MacCulloch, Diarmaid. II. Title.
DA315.F56 1997
942.05--dc20                                                    96-38921
                                                                      CIP

Set by 7 in 10/12 Sabon
Produced through Longman Malaysia, PP

# CONTENTS

# NOTE ON REFERENCING SYSTEM


Readers should note that numbers in square brackets [5] refer them to the corresponding entry in the Bibliography at the end of the book (specific page numbers are given in italics). A number in square brackets preceded by *Doc.* [*Doc.* 5] refers readers to the corresponding item in the Documents section which follows the main text.


# LIST OF MAPS

# AN INTRODUCTION TO THE SERIES

Such is the pace of historical enquiry in the modern world that there is an ever-widening gap between the specialist article or monograph, incorporating the results of current research, and general surveys, which inevitably become out of date. *Seminar Studies in History* are designed to bridge this gap. The series was founded by Patrick Richardson in 1966 and his aim was to cover major themes in British, European and World history. Between 1980 and 1996 Roger Lockyer continued his work, before handing the editorship over to Clive Emsley and Gordon Martel. Clive Emsley is Professor of History at the Open University, while Gordon Martel is Professor of International History at the University of Northern British Columbia, Canada and Senior Research Fellow at De Montfort University.

All the books are written by experts in their field who are not only familiar with the latest research but have often contributed to it. They are frequently revised, in order to take account of new information and interpretations. They provide a selection of documents to illustrate major themes and provoke discussion, and also a guide to further reading. The aim of *Seminar Studies* is to clarify complex issues without over-simplifying them, and to stimulate readers into deepening their knowledge and understanding of major themes and topics.

# PREFACES TO THE FOURTH EDITION

I am enormously grateful to Diarmaid MacCulloch for revising the text of this book. Since the third edition was published in 1983, my own research and writing interests have moved into different fields and this new edition has become well overdue. I have been fortunate in securing the collaboration of an outstanding Tudor scholar, whose work over many years has richly illuminated Tudor politics, government and society.

A.J.F., 1996

Among many others, I must thank Addison Wesley Longman for their efficiency and helpfulness in the production stages of this volume. I am particularly grateful to Mark Stoyle and Margaret Clark for their comments while I was working on the text, and to Pauline Croft, who made some invaluable last-minute suggestions, much to the book's benefit.

I was pleased to be asked to undertake the revision of a study which in its three decades of successive guises has amply proved its worth. Anthony Fletcher in his preface to the third edition of 1983 talked of the different book which he would have written if he was starting from scratch again. I am sure that this latest outcrop from his original thoughts is not the book which he was thinking of, but I am grateful to him for his tolerance of my impertinent modifications of his text. We hope that the result will be useful for a new generation of readers.

D. N. J. MacC., 1996

# PART ONE: THE BACKGROUND

## 1 THE SHAPE OF TUDOR SOCIETY

Early modern England was an unequal society, and gloried in the fact. Half a century after Queen Elizabeth's death, even the most radical groups in the upheaval of the English Civil War found it very difficult to grasp the concept of equality. The Levellers, for instance, did not conceive of political equality: their commonwealth would have excluded the very poorest sections of society from political life. Only that tiny minority, the Diggers, then began to work out the meaning of the equality of humanity, and they found few sympathisers.

If this was true for an England which had executed its king, it was truer still for the comparatively settled pre-revolutionary world. Class warfare is difficult to find there, because class warfare implies individual classes striving against each other for primacy in society: such a notion was very rare indeed in early modern Europe. The different groups in the social order were fixed for all time; social change meant not a change in the relative positions of those groups, but a change in the status of individuals, who moved from one fixed status group to another. There was only one 'class' to exercise supreme power, standing at the head of this social order; below that level, every status group could rest secure in the knowledge that it had not merely a superior group in the system, but also an inferior. The lowest in the system could hardly be considered a status group, could hardly even be conceded existence.'

Consider a contemporary snapshot of early modern society taken by a lawyer and fashionable humanist intellectual, Sir Thomas Smith. Smith wrote his descriptive tract *The Commonwealth of England* in the 1560s; he found a fourfold division in society. First of Smith's four were gentlemen. It was this class of which he spoke most, being one himself. Indeed he redivided the class into two, beginning with 'the first part of gentlemen of England called *nobilitas major*'. By this Smith meant the parliamentary peerage, that section of the landed élite who by political accidents which had largely settled down into precedent by 1500, received a regular individual summons to attend parliament in the House of Lords. Then there were 'the second sort of gentlemen which may be called *nobilitas minor*': this could in turn be subdivided in descending status order into knights, esquires and gentlemen.

Second were the citizens and burgesses: the people of the cities and towns, islands of privilege in the middle of the gentry's political world, but islands varying in size from London to some tiny and puny place which had dwindled to a village. Third were the yeomen, the prosperous middle sort of the countryside. Smith recognised their importance, perhaps more than other commentators would: he clearly felt that they were of more account than the townsmen, for he said that after the gentry, the yeoman had 'the greatest charge and doings in the commonwealth'. Last were what Smith flatly said were 'the fourth sort of men which do not rule'. In his brief account of the fourth section of society, Smith said that they 'have no voice nor authority in our commonwealth and no account is made of them, but only to be ruled, not to rule other, and yet they be not altogether neglected. For in cities and corporate towns, for default of yeomen, inquests and juries are impannelled of such manner of people. And in villages they are commonly made churchwardens, aleconners and many times constables, which office toucheth more the commonwealth, and at the first was not employed upon such low and base persons.'

Particularly from the last statement, one can see that Smith was not making a sociological analysis; he was describing power. Two further things were notable about his description. First, it wanted to be a description of a rural world; it could not ignore the towns, but they spoiled the simplicity. So Smith described the citizens as his second category, but rushed on to the yeomanry who were the natural step down the ladder from gentlemen. And amid the fourth sort, it was the towns which led the way in disturbing the natural order by spreading the load of responsibility because towns did not have yeomen. Second, there is a huge gap in the description even after Smith had talked about his fourth category. There was a large proportion of the population, cottagers, labourers, beggars, who would never come near even to the humble offices he had named. Smith had in any case more or less dismissed the fourth category of people whom he does mention: the political nation, the people who mattered, he implied, were restricted to his first three categories. This might have been just about accurate in 1560; by the eve of the English Civil War, it would be less true.

Nevertheless, Smith was right that his first three categories were the main wielders of power. Each group had its accepted sphere of operation, once more graded in hierarchical fashion. The *nobilitas major* could automatically command a say in local affairs if they wished, but their place was with the monarch in central government. Not all would wish to take up this role. A peer like Andrew Lord Windsor during the 1530s or the Earl of Derby under Elizabeth might choose to ignore the Court because he did not like the religious atmosphere. In Derby's case, this was despite the fact that he had been named a Privy Councillor; he preferred to stay in his native Lancashire building up an unchallengeable local power-base. However, there could be very serious trouble if peers who did wish to claim their place in central affairs, felt that they were being denied it. This brought Richard, Duke of York to the point of staging a *coup d'état* against Henry VI: it provoked the Northern Earls to rebellion in 1569, and led the fourth Howard Duke of Norfolk and the second Devereux Earl of Essex to the block. It has even been seen as causing the English Civil War.

The *nobilitas minor*, on the other hand, were the natural governors of the counties, with only a secondary claim on the affairs of central government. They ran the counties as justices of the peace (JPs). The counties which they ruled were groupings of the basic units of Elizabethan administration, the townships and parishes, with, in the middle of them, in an uneasy relationship, those troublesome urban chartered corporations. The townships and the parishes were the places where the yeomen held their office, as churchwardens, bailiffs, constables and the like.

Even with greater and lesser gentry reckoned together, the political leadership was a notably small group. In 1587, for instance, there were 1,500 JPs; so counting those out of political favour, plus adult sons, and a handful of powerful widows, there were about 2,500 people who mattered in central and local affairs. It was said that Queen Elizabeth could personally scrutinise the lists of actual and potential JPs for the whole country and decide on their fitness. Certainly Lord Burghley's papers show that he tried to do so. The small scale of power politics reflected the small scale of English life generally: most of the population lived in very small rural communities. London was unique in England for its size; by the early sixteenth century it was at least five times as big as Norwich, its nearest rival. Even most county towns, such as Coventry, York, Exeter or Worcester, were in the 6,000–8,000 league. England was much less urbanized than much of western Europe, but across the whole continent, for the most part, the focus of life was the local community: 'the fundamental bond, the first resort in cases of confrontation, and the most potent source of outbursts of collective violence' [11 *p. viii*].

This small scale meant that personal and political relationships were inextricably confused. Much early modern historical writing is obstinately anecdotal, and that reflects the society which wrote it: a face-to-face world. That meant that its élite had to display certain skills which are less important in government today. Tudor politics was ritualistic, and those rituals called for its leading actors to be actors in a literal sense, putting on bizarre costumes, and holding the centre of stages, moving and gesturing in particular ways. Some monarchs were incompetent at this, and lost out accordingly – for instance, Henry VI. Others, like Edward IV, Henry VIII and Elizabeth, enjoyed it, were very good at it, and benefited accordingly. Other monarchs simply disliked public theatre; a sensible monarch like Henry VII made up for being personally retiring by putting on plenty of expensive public Court display; a foolish monarch like Charles I did not bother, and enjoyed splendour away from the public arena.

The realities of sixteenth-century life increasingly disturbed official attempts to portray a harmonious and static social order. The flood of monastic, chantry and crown lands produced an open and speculative land market. The growth of the London and provincial food markets, galloping inflation and increased commercial activity and litigation offered exceptional opportunities for social mobility in Tudor England. This mobility is supported by statistical evidence for the later part of the century and was noted and commented on by contemporaries [120]. In order to preserve the ideal of a static social structure those who were successful in the competition for social advancement made frenzied efforts to conceal their movement in society by inventing pedigrees or heraldry [119]. The attitudes and standards which determined the hierarchy of social status are subtle and difficult to determine. There was sometimes disagreement when a man died as to whether his new house and prosperous farm had entitled him to move up a rung on the ladder. A man might refer to himself in his will as a yeoman but be called a husbandman by his neighbours who made the inventory of his farm. But the most important distinction in Tudor society remained that between gentry and commons. To be accepted as a gentleman a man had to be rich enough not to have to work and he had to be able to display the standard of living expected of the gentry.

The commons of Tudor England, that vast mass of the people who had no formal political role and could only bring their grievances to the attention of the government by riot or rebellion, were conventionally regarded in gentry discourse as fickle, irrational and stupid, and feared as a many-headed monster [59]. 'The people', said Archbishop Whitgift, 'are commonly bent to novelties and to factions and most ready to receive that doctrine that seemeth to be contrary to the present state and that inclineth to liberty.' The ruling class commonly claimed to regard the multitude as beneath contempt; since the aim of government propaganda in time of rebellion was to ensure the loyalty of the gentry, it was usual to emphasize the base origins of 'the rascal mob' and make little of such gentry support as the rebels maintained.

Henrician and Edwardian official publicists filled their works with much crude social hostility. There is much less evidence of it in the other direction. Where there was serious pressure of population on natural resources, or a gentleman exploited the opportunities that economic conditions offered at the expense of the commons, envy of the rich might quickly turn to open and violent anger and a sense of injustice [Doc. 18]. Expressions of class hatred are mostly isolated outbursts of rage by individuals, who usually could offer no practical course of action to back up their words; repeatedly they invoked some imagined external force, like divine intervention, or a foreign invasion. Rarely was such talk heard amid rebellions or riots [26 p. 380]. Even in time of rebellion the fundamental assumptions of Tudor society persisted: the commons expected the gentry to give the lead. If the gentry closed the gates of their parks and retired to their manor houses the commons went and sought them out. They persuaded or intimidated them into taking their side. The gentry, to their alarm, often found this assertion of their social status in rebellions decidedly provisional. In M.L. Bush's words, 'When they were compliant they were ecstatically appreciated; but the commons treated instances of independence and non-co-operation with deep suspicion and outbursts of rage' [25 p. 409]. Yet only in the case of the 1549 commotions in south-east England was hostility between the orders a major element in sixteenth-century popular disorder [Doc. 18]. The tradition of deference survived the upheavals of the century.

However, Tudor central government was conscious that this deference might not necessarily be directed to the monarch. In the north the close bonds of provincial society took additional strength from the survival until towards the end of the Tudor period of the dominance of such families as the Percies, Cliffords and Dacres, whose power, once based on livery and maintenance, continued through appointments in their households, as stewards of their lordships and as constables of their castles. The idea of faithfulness to a magnate connection survived even into the seventeenth century [66]. In 1619 Sir Henry Curwen, himself sheriff and knight of the shire in Cumberland, 'humbly tendered his service' to the ninth Earl of Northumberland from Workington, 'that place wherein many of my ancestors have been servants'. 'My ancestors', he wrote, 'always have been imployed in service in that noble house of Northumberland, and although I acknowledge myself inferior to the meanest of them, yet none of them have ever borne a more faithful affection to that famous house.'

Nevertheless, England was an unusually centralized country, and became more so in the Tudor age. In the early fifteenth century it had won an epic struggle against the Welsh leader Owain Glyn Dŵr, who had nearly deprived the English of control over the culture and society of Wales; one of the most remarkable political facts of the sixteenth century was the total lack of serious rebellion in Wales, even while the government brought the Welsh more firmly within English government and dismantled their traditional religion. Nationwide, even in the north, magnates did not pose the convincing alternative to a centralized government which was all too available in France or the Holy Roman Empire. The state of English common law, that is, royal law, is significant. Virtually every subject of the Tudor monarchs could find some way of getting a grievance into the royal courts: even the remaining villeins could usually smuggle in their cases against their theoretical lack of legal existence. This contrasts starkly with other supposedly monarchical states in Europe: in Poland, Bohemia and Hungary, for instance, the monarchy was newly excluded during the sixteenth century from jurisdiction over disputes between lords and tenants [11 *p. 52*].

# 2 IDEAS OF SUBMISSION, IDEAS OF JUSTICE

Tudor governments lacked an army with which to maintain obedience for most of the century, and even when they gained rudimentary permanent local defence forces from the 1570s, the trained bands, these could not always be relied on against local grievances [17]. They therefore needed to persuade or convince their subjects to remain passive through a generally accepted theory of obligation and submission. The need became more acute with the changes of the 1530s and the dangers attending on them. Thomas Cromwell saw the necessity of organizing and directing a group of publicists to elaborate on the theory of non-resistance expressed by William Tyndale in his *Obedience of a Christian Man* [72; 142]. He maintained close control of the printing presses, almost entirely suppressing counter-propaganda; in 1538 the import of English books printed abroad was banned. The arguments deployed by Henrician publicists, men like Richard Morison, Thomas Starkey and Robert Barnes, were taken up by those who replied to the rebels of 1549: Sir John Cheke, Thomas Cranmer and Philip Nichols [*Docs 10, 14*]. The pamphlets and ballads of Elizabeth's reign continued to echo the same themes. An account of the Tudor theory of obligation based on these writers will show how they exploited central elements of the Tudor world picture.

All moral sense and political obligation was believed to depend on religion, by which 'the whole of society was thought to be sanctioned' [111] [*Doc. 19*]. As Richard Hooker said:

> Men fearing God are thereby a great deal more effectively than by politic laws restrained from doing evil; inasmuch as those laws have no further power than over our outward actions only, whereas unto men's inward cogitations, unto the privy interests and motions of their hearts, religion serveth for a bridle.

The Royal Supremacy implied the identification of church and state. The purpose of the doctrine of the Godly Prince, elaborated by

Tudor writers, was to assert, in Richard Taverner's words, that kings 'represent unto us the person even of God himself'.

The theory of obligation employed most frequently was that of Paul's Epistle to the Romans (13:1) 'The powers that be are ordained of God.' Thus Sir John Cheke in *The Hurt of Sedition* was able to denounce the rebels of 1549 as sinning first against God, second against the King. The doctrine was one of non-resistance rather than obedience because it was usually qualified by a paraphrase of the apostle Peter's statement in Acts 5:29 that 'We ought to obey God rather than men.' Robert Barnes maintained that powers must be suffered 'always provided that they repugn not against the Gospel nor destroy our faith'. But little emphasis was put on this qualification. It was much more common to stress, as Hugh Latimer did in one of his sermons, that it might be the will of God that a sinful man should suffer under tyrants.

> If the king should require of thee an unjust request, yet art thou bound to pay it and not to resist and rebel . . . the king indeed is in peril of his soul for asking of an unjust request; and God will in His due time reckon with him for it: but thou must not take upon thee to judge him. . . . And know this, that whensoever there is any unjust exaction laid upon thee it is a plague and punishment for thy sin.

But the powers that be were not just political. Everyone was expected to obey their immediate superior. 'The rule of obedience', said Archbishop Whitgift, 'that is betwixt the magistrate and the subject holdeth betwixt the husband and the wife, the father and his child, the master and the servant.' It is this idea which connects the theory of obligation, based on Romans, with the doctrine of the Great Chain of Being, the most persuasive foundation for a theory of non-resistance available to the Tudor writer. The idea of the Great Chain of Being was well expressed by the fifteenth-century jurist Sir John Fortescue:

> God created as many different kinds of things as he did creatures, so that there is no creature which does not differ in some respect superior or inferior to all the rest. So that from the highest angel down to the lowest of his kind there is absolutely not found an angel that has not a superior and inferior; nor from man down to the meanest worm is there any creature which is not in some respect superior to one creature and inferior to another. So that there is nothing which the bond of order does not embrace.

The Great Chain of Being's existence was a commonplace for those who lived in Tudor England. The metaphor 'served to express the unimaginable plentitude of God's creation, its unfaltering order and its ultimate unity' [129 *pp. 37–8*]. The principle of degree dominated people's imaginations. Order among humans corresponded to the order of the cosmos, as traditionally understood. Shakespeare assumed the interconnections of 'the heavens themselves, the planets, and this centre'; in each he saw hierarchy and place.

How could communities,
Degrees in schools and brotherhoods in cities,
Peaceful commerce from dividable shores,
The primogenitive and due of birth,
Prerogative of age, crowns, sceptres, laurels,
But by degree stand in authentic place?

asked Ulysses in his speech on degree in *Troilus and Cressida*. The Great Chain of Being meant interdependence as well as authority; all authorities in it held their power for the good of their inferiors and subject to their superiors. William Gouge said

They that are superiors to some are inferiors to others. . . . The master that hath servants under him, may be under the authority of a magistrate. Yea, God hath so disposed every one's several place, as there is not any one, but in some respect is under another, and all under the king. The king himself is under God.

This was why, as Protector Somerset explained to the western rebels, there must be a difference between 'the harte and wordes of a king enoincted that ruleth by counsell and kepeth his Realme in defence and quyetnes' and the 'blinde guides of Sedition and uprore'. The ideal was one of harmony and cooperation: 'We are all members of one body; and we know we have need one of another. The Lord cannot want the help of the toe, though the least and lowest member', wrote Edwin Sandys. The image of the commonwealth as a human body was a favourite one with Tudor publicists. Morison used it to show the absurdity of rebellion and explained that it was for the welfare of society as a whole that while some must rule others must work: 'These must not go, arme in arme, but the one before, the other behynde' [*Doc. 10*]. Here, as so often in Tudor political writing, Morison was paraphrasing and expanding on a biblical passage, in this case 1 Corinthians 12:12.

Rebellion upset both the social and the political order. 'God hath made the poore, and hath made them to be poore', wrote Cheke, 'that he myght shew his might, and set them aloft when he listeth, for such cause as to hym seemeth and plucke downe the riche, to hys state of povertie to shew his power.' 'Where there is any lack of order', said Sir Thomas Elyot, 'needs must be perpetual conflict.' The Great Chain theory was strongly reflected in the *Homily of Obedience*, one of the set of twelve official sermons issued and ordered to be read in churches in 1547: 'Where there is no right order there reigneth all abuse, carnal liberty, enormity, sin and babylonical confusion' [49 *p. 15*]. A useful appeal could be made to the image of order presented in the family. So Lord Russell was urged, in Protector Somerset's orders on the quashing of the 1549 Western Rebellion, to give special charge to masters and fathers to have 'an earnest continual regard to the good governance of their children and servants'.

At its crudest and most exaggerated, government propaganda appealed to the dread of anarchy with which people were obsessed. The *Homily of Obedience* described the 'mischief and utter destruction' that would ensue without kings and magistrates: 'No man shall sleep in his house or bed unkilled.' Philip Nichols pointed out to the western rebels in 1549 'the universal desolation of your own selves' that they could expect [*Doc. 14*]. Morison, in his *Lamentation*, painted a vivid picture of the results of sedition: virgins ravished, death, robbery and spoil. He went on to ask how anyone could deliberately reduce the country to such a state. Morison's treatises were intended to rally the support of the gentry in the crisis of the Henrician Reformation. So he appealed directly to their insecurity in the face of the multitude: 'Howe many gentyllmen for lacke of their ventes shalbe fayn to lay their landes to mortgage?' Morison saw rebellion in harsh economic terms. Even 'in time of peace be not all men almost at war with them that be rich?' he once wrote. His emphasis in *A Remedy of Sedition* is on the threat to wealth and property 'whan every man wyll rule' [46, *pp. 200–2*]. He is here almost Marxist in his analysis [*Doc. 10*].

In 1536 and again in 1549 the threat that enemies abroad would use England's weakness to invade caused the government considerable anxiety. In both cases it became an important argument in their propaganda. 'If Lincolnshire seke to distroye Englande, what wonder is hit if Fraunce and Scotlande sometime have fought to offende me?' asked Morison. In these passages he appealed directly to the 'men of Lincolnshire' though it was highly unlikely that copies of his books would come into the hands of the rebels themselves. He used the image of the ship of state, familiar in political theory, to drive home his point: 'What folly, what madnes is this, to make an hole in the shyppe that thou saylest in?' Somerset in a letter to the western rebels in 1549 concentrated on warning them of the disastrous consequences of 'your owne foly and sturdines'. The French were rumoured to be preparing an attack on the Scilly Isles: 'Yf they shulde descend and take place wolde not they then rob and spoile pill and subdue you?' He told the Devon justices to employ the same argument [*Doc. 15*].

Frequently, history was used to show (inaccurately) how rebellions had always failed in the past. Archbishop Cranmer provided Old Testament examples in his sermon on rebellion in 1549, describing the fate of the children of Israel who rebelled against Moses. He brought his message home with more immediate cases and maintained that following the failure of the peasants' war in Germany, in 1525, over 100,000 rebels were killed in three months. Richard Morison in his *Lamentation* catalogued the rebels who had failed in the fourteenth and fifteenth centuries. He reminded his readers of the way Henry VII had dealt with the Cornishmen on Blackheath field only thirty-nine years before.

The problem for Tudor governments was that such popular clichés could be turned in other directions. The theme of loyalty and obligation worked downwards as well as upwards: the Great Chain of Being imposed duties on superiors as well as inferiors. The relationship of landlord and tenant was a prime cohesive force in Tudor society. It was a relationship involving responsibilities on both sides, and contained a strong moral element. Sir John Gostwick's memorandum of advice to his heir on estate management, written in 1540, shows his concern to retain his credit as a good landlord and to do well by God and the king. He told his successor not to increase his tenants' rents unless they were imposing increases on their own subtenants [*39 p. 161*]. Many rebellions saw their task as calling social superiors back to their obligations: often calling on the king to redress the misdeeds of the nobility and gentry. Other commotions, as noted in Chapter 1 above, paradoxically acknowledged the hierarchy of society by intimidating social superiors into playing the roles of leaders in rebellion.

Dangerously ambiguous in troubled times was the cliché of 'commonwealth': did it refer to the whole realm, as when government spokesmen expressed their concern for the commonwealth, and prepared schemes of reform to benefit it? It might equally refer only to the commons without the gentry and nobility, as seems to be the case in the title of 'the Pilgrimage of Grace for the commonwealth' in 1536 [25 *p. 396*]. Here was a word which the government could only try to reserve for its own purposes, but it was difficult to defuse this explosive idea's power to arouse popular feeling and crystallize indignation. In 1536, one of the Suffolk bailiffs of the Duke of Suffolk, Henry VIII's own commander against the Lincolnshire rebels, vowed not to 'fyght ageynst hys cosyns and kyndred ... the good cristen men of Yngland were in [the] North, and [thei] were than rysyn for common welth' [52 *p. 76*].

The Great Chain of Being was not the only conventional way of viewing the mechanism of the cosmos. Equally compelling was the idea of the wheel of fortune, a circular notion of time, in which the mighty could be brought low and the humble exalted – a theme which was, after all, to be found in the *Magnificat* heard in Cranmer's evensong service. Equally biblical, although common through classical literature as well, was the notion of the golden age in remote time. Through the wheel of fortune this age might be restored, and popular action might help the restoration on its way. Sometimes this could be linked to some figure in the past who represented justice, often a king who had been carried off in the prime of life: so Perkin Warbeck and Lambert Simnel were able to carry out their impersonations of deceased Yorkist princes, and stories of the return of Edward VI circulated in the reign of Mary.

Rarely do we hear coherent schemes of such views expressed in rebellions, for no one had the sort of resources available to the government to publicize them. However, very frequent are reports of prophecies which were attributed to mythical or historical figures and then used to make sense of a contemporary crisis. The government in the religious upheavals in the 1530s even tried to exploit such prophecies to justify what it was doing, but in the end it realized that this was too dangerous a tactic to follow, because prophecies could equally well be a justification for opposition: determined efforts at suppression followed [71; 51 *pp. 78–81*]. Popular opinion could take paths of its own, and was not always easily manipulated, despite all the government's advantages in publicity. The vital fact for Tudor monarchs to remember was the price of obedience for those who demanded it: good governance and justice for all the members of the commonwealth.

# PART TWO: DESCRIPTIVE ANALYSIS

## 3 TAXATION AND REBELLION

It was an accepted principle that the king should only tax his people for the needs of war or in other exceptional circumstances, and through the consent of parliament. In fact an Act of 1483 declared that non-parliamentary taxation was illegal. Parliamentary opposition to taxation concentrated on restricting the total amount granted and the way in which the money should be levied and spent. However, in their search for ways of extending England's antiquated tax system beyond the fifteenth and tenth, the early Tudors determinedly pressed parliament into granting a new form of taxation levied not by traditional fixed valuations of whole communities, but on regular reassessments of individuals: these taxes were known as subsidies. They fell hard on the poorer section of the community. It is significant that in 1489 and 1497, and again in 1536, it was a subsidy rather than a fifteenth and tenth that caused anger.

The House of Commons' growing distrust of the crown's financial motives is illustrated by their insistence in 1497, following the Treaty of Etaples five years before, that parts of their grants should be dependent on the crown actually undertaking specified military expeditions. In 1523 the opposition to Wolsey's subsidy demands was prolonged and heated. But even then no one, unless Cromwell did actually deliver the speech which survives in the hand of one of his clerks, went so far as to question Henry VIII's grand design against France [38 p. 19].

At the local level popular dislike of taxation was expressed in sporadic outbreaks of violence against tax collectors – the murder at Taunton in late 1497, for instance, of the man widely seen as Henry VII's west-country agent in the taxes which had provoked open rebellion earlier that year [2 p. 9]. In the period 1485–1547 there were eleven recorded cases of assaults on tax collectors, concentrated around London and the south coast, and there were probably others which never reached the courts. More common and more widely spread geographically are cases of the forcible rescue of goods, seized by a tax commissioner from a man who had refused to pay; at least 112 such cases are recorded [114]. It is against this background that we must examine the more determined resistance to taxation in this period. Twice, in 1489 and 1497, this amounted to rebellion and was ruthlessly crushed. Twice, in 1513 and 1525, the resistance was passive and succeeded.

## THE YORKSHIRE REBELLION, 1489

The rebellion in Yorkshire in April 1489 arose from the efforts of the fourth Percy Earl of Northumberland, who was Lieutenant General of the Middle and Eastern Marches, to collect the subsidy for that year. This was a new levy, which had been granted by parliament to enable Henry VII to intervene on behalf of Brittany against the French crown [58 *pp. 51–2*]. Northumberland heard of a gathering from Cleveland who were resolved to protest, and he marched to meet them; he was assassinated at South Kilvington, near Thirsk – the only person killed in the entire rising [58 *p. 44*]. The growing armed crowds which coalesced under the leadership of Sir John Egremont galvanized the king into raising a large army to march north. The massive scale of his reaction unnerved the rebels, who dispersed as the advance guard under the Earl of Surrey arrived at York, and further action became unnecessary [10 *pp. 38–41, 52–5*].

For all Henry's fears of another dynastic attempt to destroy him, the rising seems to have been a genuine expression of popular anger about war taxation. Other elements are more fugitive in the record. Polydore Vergil and the Great Chronicle of London mention the rebels' sympathy with the Yorkist cause, which is indicated by the participation of Egremont. A quotation from a proclamation which survives among the Paston Letters says that the rebels intended 'to geynstonde such persons as is abowtwarde for to dystroy owre suffereyn Lorde the Kynge and the Commons of Engelond for suche unlawfull poyntes as Seynt Thomas of Cauntyrbery dyed for'. 'Unlawfull' is probably a hostile addition by Paston, but this is probably evidence that Becket was remembered in popular folklore for his stand against the king for church privilege. The reference might be to the Act of 1489 on benefit of clergy, but is more plausibly explained by popular anger at Henry VII's increasing infringements of northern sanctuaries in order to round up his political opponents [58 *pp. 52–3*]. M.L. Bush, however, suggests that it may be yet another reference to unlawful taxation; St Thomas was commonly associated with resistance to Henry II's plans for taxes on the poor [22 *p. 395*].

The accounts of the assassination in Skelton's elegy on Northumberland and William Peeris's Percy chronicle emphasize the nobility's horror at servants' treachery: the Earl was abandoned by his retinue, 'those to whom he gave fees and was right speciall lord'. Northumberland had been left dangerously exposed to the anger of his social inferiors by the king's ruthless determination to impose his will on the provinces in order to raise the cash he wanted. The first Tudor, his formative years spent in Brittany and France, was unfamiliar with the careful compromises and structures of consent on which English government rested. It was left to him to pick up the pieces of northern government during the minority of the next Percy Earl, by establishing a council for the north in the name of his own baby son. The young prince's real lieutenant, the Earl of Surrey, despite being a southerner, proved a great success in binding the north to the Tudor dynasty [10 *p. 48*].

## THE CORNISH REBELLION, 1497

In 1497 it was Cornwall that began a rebellion. Henry wanted money for an army to deal with Perkin Warbeck, who had received a ready welcome from James IV of Scotland. In all, in one subsidy and two fifteenths and tenths, parliament granted the king £120,000. This was far more than was paid in any other year of the reign, and additionally a forced loan had just been levied. Only in 1492, when £56,311 was paid in taxation, did the yield of parliamentary grants exceed £31,000 [*114; 2 p. 4*]. The burden affected most of the population, who could see no overwhelming threat from Scotland. For the Cornish in particular, the problem of the north seemed much too remote. They were encouraged to resist by an able Bodmin lawyer, Thomas Flamank.

Persuaded by Flamank to direct their resentment against the king's 'evil advisers' Cardinal Morton and Sir Reginald Bray, the Cornishmen made a remarkable march across England to present their grievances to the government. They were led by Flamank and Michael Joseph An Gof, a blacksmith from the Lizard area; clergy and well-established Cornish gentry joined them. The march was orderly. Devon seems mostly to have remained aloof, perhaps because of its traditional antagonism to the Cornish, but prominent Somerset gentry and clergy aided the rebels, judging by the royal fines afterwards [2, *pp. 6, 10*]. At Wells they gained the support of Lord Audley, an impoverished and discontented nobleman, whom, says Polydore Vergil, they 'with acclamation accepted as their chief'. They met with little resistance as they marched across England: no doubt many sympathized with their protest, and once more the fines after the rebellion suggest that many joined them. It was the most frightening variety of rebellion for a Tudor monarch: a cry of anger which crossed social barriers in the West Country.

Henry had been caught unawares; by 13 June the Cornishmen and their allies, said to number 15,000, were at Guildford. The army of 8,000 that was being prepared against Scotland under Lord Daubeney had to be rapidly diverted. After a brief encounter between 500 of Daubeney's spearmen and the rebels near Guildford, the insurgents continued their march round the south of London. Meanwhile the king himself gathered forces at Henley and on 16 June was able to join Daubeney, who was protecting the approaches to the city. The London chronicler tells how 'the king was seen in the feelde, and abrewyng and comfortyng of his people'. The same day the rebel army came up to Blackheath where at last they could look down on London. Many were disillusioned by their failure to attract support in Kent, and lost heart when they found the leaders were preparing for battle. Guns were placed to defend the passage of the river at Deptford. The London chronicler relates how the rebel camp was 'all that night in greate agony and variaunce; ffor some of thym were mynded to have comyn to the Kyng and to have yolded theym and put theym fully in his mercy and grace; but the smith was of the contrary myende'. A large number did desert and only about 10,000 were left to face the army, said to number 25,000, that the king had mustered.

Henry not only concentrated overwhelming forces but planned his attack meticulously, sending a force of archers and cavalry round the back of the rebels. Ten years before he had only defeated Lambert Simnel at Stoke after a stiff three-hour contest. This time he wanted a quick and crushing victory. After Daubeney had gained the Deptford bridge he was taken prisoner, but released almost at once. Bacon concludes the story, or at least the sanitized official version which the Tudors allowed to survive: 'The Cornishmen, being ill-armed and ill-led and without horse or artillery, were with no great difficulty cut in pieces and put to flight.' The king entered the city over London bridge and was received by the mayor, 'to whom he gave cherefull thankes for his good diligence of kepyng and orderyng of the Citie . . . and from thens rode unto Powlis and there offred'.

Many of the rebels died on the field. Audley was executed and Flamank and Joseph were hanged, drawn and quartered. Henry cancelled an order that their dismembered bodies should be exhibited throughout Cornwall through fear of the rumours that the country was 'still eager to promote a revolution if they were in anyway provoked'. But he proceeded to fine all those involved in the rebellion with systematic and unprecedented severity. He took in all from the Cornishmen and Devonians, including Warbeck's adherents later in the year, about £15,000, and more from a swathe of counties on the rebels' route to London [2 *pp. 6–9, 12–13*].'The less blood he drew', said Francis Bacon of the first Tudor king, 'the more he took of treasure.' The strategy worked: Cornwall would not cause serious trouble for the Tudors again until 1548.

RESISTANCE TO TAXATION, 1513–25

It was not until 1513, as Henry VIII resumed a costly series of wars with France and Scotland, that people again found themselves expected to pay a subsidy and a fifteenth and tenth in the same year. The total yield of parliamentary taxation levied in this year was £62,126. Polydore Vergil provides the only account of the passive resistance in Yorkshire. He noted that the 'sudden new upheaval of the north country folk' was caused 'by the heaviness of the tax imposed a little earlier'. As in 1497 the burden imposed by the government was exceptional. According to Vergil 'these north country folk volunteered their personal services in waging war, but they refused the money because they have so little of it'. His account is confirmed by evidence that the commissioners for collecting the subsidy in the West Riding wapentakes of Staincliffe and Ewcross had difficulty in making their assessments, which ought to have been returned by early summer [118 *pp. 198–9*]. They were not finally returned until 1515 and the towns of Dent and Sedbergh still refused to appear in January of that year. The general poverty of these wapentakes is not in doubt. The king accepted a petition from nineteen towns and villages and remitted entirely their payment of the fifteenth and tenth.

In 1523, in order to pay for the king's grandiose foreign policy, Wolsey put before parliament heavier financial demands than the commons had ever faced or envisaged: £800,000. The commons, Hall relates, said 'the sum was impossible to be levied'. They argued with some sense that if such a sum of ready money was taken by the king, the economy would collapse: 'Then men must barter clothe for vitaille and bread for cheese and so one thyng for another.' In fact Wolsey had probably pitched his demand high as a bargaining ploy [34 *pp. 1–5*]. The subsidy, phased over four years and collected at much lower rates than first sought, yielded £151,215. The major part of this, £136,578, had been collected by the spring of 1525. It was at this moment, when the country had just paid out the largest grant in taxation of the whole period 1485–1543, that Wolsey sent out commissioners to collect the Amicable Grant. He was desperate for money to satisfy the king's urge to grasp the opportunity offered by the defeat of France at Pavia.

The Amicable Grant belied its name, and the name's novelty was an unhappy witness to the tax's novelty. It was a levy of between one-sixth and one-tenth on the goods of the laity and one-third on the goods of the clergy. Wolsey's idea was to extend the benevolences which Edward IV had extracted from the wealthy and which (as a London councillor had reminded him) the Act of 1483 had forbidden, to the country as a whole. Commissions to collect the grant were sent out on 21 March to senior lay or clerical figures in each county, and they ordered that the bulk of the money should be collected by Whitsuntide (4–6 June): a startlingly short time. Moreover, the second instalment of the 1523 subsidy had not fully been collected yet [14 *pp. 191–2*].

Trouble was inevitable and was indeed anticipated in the commission. Archbishop Warham reported on 12 April that he found the Kentish clergy 'not inclined to the grant' and that heads of religious houses had answered 'that they cannot contribute as they are required'. People who said they simply had not the money may have been honest. At Ely they said they would gladly sell their cattle and goods 'but no man in the country has money to buy or lend'. 'Some who at the first loan were well off now are not worth a groat when their debts are paid.' At Norwich the wealthy aldermen could offer plate but not money. The Duke of Norfolk explained to Wolsey the plight of the large population of the poor who depended on worsted and strawmaking and were paid weekly [106].

In a letter of 5 April, Warham gave Wolsey a full account of the arguments and attitudes he had encountered, and with which he may have sympathized. The whole policy of the French war was now called into question. There was no enthusiasm for continental expeditions. People regretted the captivity of Francis I, the money that had been spent to no purpose on futile expeditions and the king's ambition to win France: Henry VIII 'hath not one foot of land more in France than his most noble father hadd, which lakked no riches or wisdom to wyne the kingdome of France if he had thought it expedient. . . . And if the King win France, he will be obliged to spend his time and revenues there.' Wolsey was the scapegoat but resentment also fell on Warham. He had been called an old fool behind his back for consenting to the grant, he told Wolsey. Anticlericalism was an element of danger: 'Some malicious persons say that it would be better for an old fool like him to take his beads in his hand, than to meddle in temporal business pertaining to war and general undoing of this country' [13 *p. 99*].

The collection of the grant made no progress during April. One of the counties where passive resistance was strongest was Warwickshire. On 28 April the government granted the whole shire remission from the grant, admitting that the people's 'powers and abilities' there 'be not correspondent and egall to their good willes . . . nor ther be able to make unto us payment of the sayd grannte without their extreme detryment and excessive hinderaunce' [104 *p. 63*].

Reports from East Anglia, Berkshire, Wiltshire and Kent were equally depressing. On 26 April Wolsey told the London councillors that, on the king's advice, he would demand no fixed sums but such as they would willingly grant. When the rumour of his retreat spread in East Anglia the mood of the people hardened. On 8 May the Earl of Essex reported from Stanstead that he had met with determined resistance. After an assembly of 1,000 persons on the Suffolk border, he had suspended proceedings till he heard the king's pleasure: 'Some fear to be hewn in pieces if they make any grant, and there is great danger of more insurrections.'

The most serious rising was in the Lavenham and Sudbury area of Suffolk. Faced with a band of 4,000, the Dukes of Norfolk and Suffolk treated the affair cautiously and leniently [*Doc. 1*]. Lavenham had paid a total of £354 1s 4d (£354.07) in the subsidy payments of 1524 and 1525 but a large proportion of this was contributed by rich clothiers, including the Spring family. The wage-earners there numbered just over half the taxable population yet owned less than 3 per cent of the property. In 1525 it seems many of these men were out of work so it was impossible for them to answer the king's demand. The bulk of those involved in the cloth-producing communities around Lavenham were the poorest inhabitants, revealing a social gap between them and the wealthy minority. However, they joined with purely agricultural villages, from which an impressive cross-section of society from wealthy to poor took part in the protest [86 *pp. 294–6*].

Wolsey replied to the duke's report by urging strong measures. However, when the four 'principal offenders' he had arrested were brought to London, Henry showed his political sense by bowing before the storm. He abandoned the grant. At 'a great counsaill', relates Hall, 'he openly said that his mind was not to ask anything of his commons which might sound to his dishonour or to the breach of his laws'. When the king inquired how the commissioners' demands came to be so strict 'the Cardinal excused himself'. At the end of May the ringleaders were brought before Star Chamber and pardoned after they had been 'shown their offences, with terrible words'. Wolsey led an ostentatious ceremony of reconciliation, begging the king for pardon for fellow-Suffolk men, and even supplying them with more than enough cash to cover their time in gaol [86, *p. 293; 113 pp. 135–9*].

The resistance to the Amicable Grant made Henry realise that in the last resort his kingship rested on his partnership with the tax-paying classes. He found himself up against the vocally expressed public opinion of south-east England, of the counties on which the strength of Tudor monarchy rested. The affair had begun with propaganda. The commissioners had been told to make solemn processions and bonfires in celebration of the French king's defeat before they began collecting the money. It ended in open retreat. Tudor monarchs always found it needed discussion and concession to obtain taxes from parliament. On this occasion the government found itself proceeding from persuasion to concession in face of extra-parliamentary opinion. It may not be entirely irrelevant that Hall noted in his chronicle for 1525 that 'in this troublous season the uplandish men of Germany rose in a great number, almost an hundred thousand, and rebelled against the princes of Germany'.

Popular opinion had made a significant impact on foreign policy. Henry was forced to abandon his schemes for European hegemony, and peace with France was the only course. When in the 1540s he again became involved in large-scale continental commitments, the gentry made large grants of taxation. But, if Henry had not been dispensing monastic lands to attract their loyalty, he might have found the taxpayers unwilling again then. The total yield of parliamentary taxes in the period 1541–47 was £656,245. Even bearing in mind the beginnings of the inflation, this is an astounding figure. In the whole of Henry VII's reign the country had paid only £282,000, and in the period 1509–40 the total came to £520,463. Despite the resistance to taxation that has been discussed in this chapter, the development of the subsidy must be rated a spectacular (if temporary) achievement by the early Tudors. The historian of parliamentary taxation in this period has concluded of Henry VIII's demands in the 1540s, probably the heaviest taxation since the fourteenth century, 'such was the political cohesion between the leading social classes and the crown that the former displayed an unparalleled willingness to operate a system of taxation, which, for its sophistication and attention to the principles of distributive justice, was several centuries ahead of its time' [115 *p. 255*]. However, he also notes that after 1547, when Henry's powerful personality was no longer regulating the system, standards of assessment rapidly dropped, particularly for the wealthier classes.

# 4 THE PILGRIMAGE OF GRACE

## THE LINCOLNSHIRE RISING

Three government commissions were at work in Lincolnshire at Michaelmas in 1536. That for dissolving the smaller monasteries had been in the county since June, a second commission was assessing and collecting the subsidy and a third was appointed to enquire into the fitness and education of the clergy. They worked in an atmosphere of rumour and alarm. It was said that jewels and plate were to be confiscated from parish churches, that all gold was to be taken to the mint to be tested, and that taxes were to be levied on all horned cattle, and on christenings, marriages and burials. There were even wilder rumours: 'that there shall be no church within five miles, and that all the rest shall be put down', that people would not be allowed to eat white bread, goose or capon without paying a tribute to the king. It was said that every man would have to give an account of his property and income and a false return would lead to forfeiture of all his goods. There is evidence that these rumours had spread to many parts of the eastern and midland counties by the autumn of 1536. But they were strongest in Lincolnshire. The rising there, based on the three towns of Louth, Caistor and Horncastle, was an outburst by people who, as Wriothesley told Cromwell, 'think they shall be undone for ever' [68].

The rising began at Louth, where the people were immensely proud of the magnificent spire of their church completed only twenty years before. When the Bishop of Lincoln's registrar arrived there on 2 October to carry out the visitation of the clergy, he was seized by some townsmen who had been guarding the treasure house of the church all the night before. They were led by the shoemaker Nicholas Melton ('Captain Cobbler') whose armed supporters were paid from church funds. These men made the registrar and the assembled priests swear on oath to be true to them, and burnt the registrar's papers. Then they marched to Legbourne nunnery and captured the royal commissioners who were at work there.

The Louth outburst was the signal for a rising throughout the county. Melton disregarded a message that reached him on 2 October that Yorkshire was not ready to rise and ordered a muster for the next day. On 3 October the commission for the subsidy was due to meet at Caistor. The priests of the neighbourhood were there also to attend the commissary's court. The commons were alarmed by a rumour that their weapons were going to be confiscated and the priests feared their examination. The commissioners hoped to reason with the people but when the commons of Louth, 3,000 strong, came in sight they turned their horses and fled. Some of the commissioners then joined the rising. That evening four of them signed a letter to the king requesting a general pardon for the assembly caused by the 'common voice and fame . . . of newe enhaunscments and other importunate charges'.

By 4 October the gentry had assumed leadership roles in the rising. Their involvement gave the movement an air of legitimacy, transforming it from a plebeian riot into a demonstration, constrained throughout by respect for established authority including that of the king, against certain of his policies [68]. By 10 October the gentry leaders were writing to the king's commander, the Duke of Suffolk, claiming that their strategy was to divert the commons' energy into petitioning and waiting for an answer at Lincoln, rather than marching further south [61 *pp. 58–9, 65–6*]. Nevertheless, willingly or unwillingly, they were at first deeply implicated in the spreading troubles. In north Lincolnshire gentry mobilized their own wapentakes through the machinery of musters; at Horncastle gentlemen appeared at a rebel rally 'well harnassed with their tenants'. When Dr Raynes, the hated chancellor of the Bishop of Lincoln, was brought to the Horncastle muster on 4 October the frenzied mob set upon him and murdered him with their staves. It was left to the sheriff to divide his clothes and the money in his purse among the crowd. It was on this occasion that the first manifesto of the rising was drawn up [*Doc. 2*].

At least 10,000 people marched to Lincoln. Lord Hussey, one of the county's senior noblemen, hoped to mediate between the dissidents and the Court, manoeuvred, hesitated and finally, on 7 October, fled the county; younger peers, Lord Clinton and Burgh, had already found that their tenants would not fight against the insurgents, and so had made their escape [*52 pp. 73–7*; 68]. Since many other heads of ancient landed families, who as JPs were responsible for order in the shire, had thrown in their lot with the rising, there was no one to stop its progress. The parish clergy played a crucial role in mobilizing the movement and monks from Barlings, Bardney and Kirkstead joined the rebel host, horsed and armed.

At Lincoln a new set of articles was drawn up and sent to London. The gentry had difficulty in restraining the commons' impatient demand to proceed south to the general muster planned to take place at Ancaster, near Grantham, on 8 October. When the king's reply, threatening extreme punishment if the rebels did not disperse at once, reached Lincoln on 10 October, the royal army under the Duke of Suffolk was already only forty miles away at Stamford. For the principal gentry involved this was the moment of choice. Any further resistance was treason. They decided to sue for pardon and told the commons they would not go forward. At this there was bitter recrimination against the gentry and the rising faltered. When Lancaster Herald arrived at Lincoln on 11 October, he persuaded the commons to go home: the Duke of Suffolk's refusal to negotiate while they were still in arms had caused general dismay [61 *p. 66*]. Nevertheless, the crowds only dispersed after promises from the gentry to muster them again if the royal pardon did not become operative, and there was serious unrest in the county for several weeks after the dispersal [52 *p. 66*].

When the people of Horncastle reached home they placed the banner they had designed for themselves in church; its complex symbolism is difficult for us to unravel with certainty. The Five Wounds of Christ proclaimed that the commons fought in Christ's cause: what of the other symbols, a chalice with the host, a plough, a horn? These might be taken as emblems of grievance: the chalice standing for the commons' fear that church plate was going to be confiscated, the plough for the impact of enclosure for pasture on the husbandman, the horn for the rumoured tax on horned cattle. Alternatively, we could read these as claims of support from all three estates: the clergy (chalice), the commons (plough) and nobility (hunting-horn) – one could plausibly also refer the horn to Horncastle's community name. Perhaps we should not seek one single meaning.

Accounts of the balance of leadership in the rising are precisely contradictory. One eye-witness described how the people 'did nothing but by the gentlemen's commandment, and they durst never stir in the field from the place they were appointed till the gentlemen directed them what to do'; yet another said that 'as farforth as he knows, the gentylmen ware taken ageynst there willys, and was fayne to go with commons and to do as they dyd for fere of there lyvys' [*52 p. 54*]. The deposition of Nicholas Leche seems to show that at Horncastle the gentry took the lead in 'harnessing' themselves, as well as in drawing up the first set of articles, but he had compelling self-interest in saying this [*Doc. 2*]. Nicholas Melton, another rebel leader below the level of the gentry, apparently always had his suspicions of his gentry allies: he exclaimed in prison, 'What whorsones were we that we had not killed the gentlemen, for I thought allwayes that they would be traytors' [*61 p. 72*]. The gentry claimed to the Duke of Suffolk that they were deliberately delaying the rebels' progress, and if this was indeed their deliberate strategy, the collapse of morale at Lincoln would seem to have vindicated them.

THE PILGRIMAGE: OCTOBER–DECEMBER 1536

The first stirrings in the north actually predated the Lincolnshire explosion: around 25 September oath-taking began among the commons in the Lordship of Dent in the West Riding of Yorkshire [*25 p. 249*]. However, the Dent oath-taking only gradually spread its catchment area over three weeks, and the gatherings which eventually far outclassed the Lincolnshire stirs in their range and seriousness began far to the east of Dent, at Beverley in the East Riding. This was on 8 October, a week after Lincolnshire had risen. Already prominent was the name of Robert Aske: a letter from Aske was made public at Beverley, bidding every man to swear to be true to God, the king and the commonwealth and to maintain the Holy Church.

Aske was an astute and successful lawyer who had a number of grievances against the Cromwellian regime, and who had already become one of the gentry captains in Lincolnshire [*25 pp. 28, 81*]. He was very probably involved in some kind of a conspiracy to mount a northern rising before Lincolnshire stirred. On 10 October the ringing of church bells brought out West Riding Marshland and East Riding Howdenshire, and Aske took authority as the chief captain there: forming the people into companies, he organized the daily musters. Other local gentry were persuaded by popular pressure to follow his lead. On 13 October the companies from the East Riding and Marshland joined up on their march to York. It seems to have been during the advance to York that Aske began to speak of the rising as a pilgrimage, telling two messengers 'they were pilgrims and had a pilgrimage gate to go'. The full title of the rising became 'The Pilgrimage of Grace for the commonwealth': the grace which it sought was not primarily grace from God, but grace from the king for his poor subjects [*25 p. 119*].

On 16 October, already possibly 10,000 strong, the Pilgrims made a triumphant entry to the city where the commons had declared for them several days before. When the mayor yielded, Aske sent him a copy of the Pilgrims' Articles [*Doc. 3*]. Their programme at this stage was substantially that of the Lincolnshire rebels, whose articles had circulated in Marshland. His idealistic conception of the rising emerged fully in his second proclamation, issued once he was in possession of York:

> For thys pylgrymage we have taken hyt for the preservacyon of Crystes churche, of thys realme of England, the kynge our soverayne lord, the nobylytie and comyns of the same, and to the entent to macke petycion to the kynges highnes for the reformacyon of that whyche is amysse within thys hys realme.

Aske emphasized the Pilgrims' peaceful intentions, saying they meant no 'malys dysplesure to noo persons but suche as be not worthy to remayne nyghe abowte the kynge oure soverayne lordes personne'; yet he maintained also their determination to 'fyght and dye agaynst all those that shalbe abowte towardes to stope us'.

Once in the city, Aske took careful precautions against spoil, not allowing any footmen within the walls. He ensured that goods obtained were paid for. He posted on the door of the Minster a plan agreed by the captains for the restoration of religious houses. In the city, this meant restoring two small Benedictine houses suppressed that summer: Holy Trinity and the nunnery of St Clement's, together with the nearby Augustinians at Healaugh Priory [*102 pp. 50, 235*]. Hull capitulated to the rebels on 19 October. Meanwhile Lord Darcy in Pontefract Castle, known as 'the key to the north', did nothing. He wrote long and desperate appeals to Henry. The castle, he reported on 13 October, had 'not one gun in it ready to shoot' and was 'much out of frame'. Four days later he found himself cut off from the town, which had risen in sympathy with the Pilgrimage.

During the same week that the East Riding rose, about 11 October, Richmondshire, Mashamshire, Sedbergh and Nidderdale also mustered, occupying Jervaulx Abbey and restoring Coverham

**The Pilgrimage of Grace**
**—1536—**

0    25    50 km

N

+     Monasteries involved in the Pilgrimage
•••••••••▸   Route of Lincolnshire rebels
————▸   Main routes of Yorkshire rebels
– – – –▸   Route of Kirkby Stephen and Cumberland rebels
—•—•—▸   Route of Westmorland rebels

*Map 1*

Abbey. The North Riding company held a series of assemblies at Richmond, at which they swore in various gentlemen as their leaders. These included the natural leaders of local society, Lord Latimer and Sir Christopher Danby, but the major figure emerging by 15 October was Robert Bowes. As a lawyer and younger son of a gentry family, Bowes was of similar status to Robert Aske, and he seems to have had a similar dynamic influence on what became the most influential of all the various regional hosts. The Richmond assemblies were responsible for instigation and coordination of the risings to the north, issuing calls to the commons in the Palatinate of Durham, Westmorland and Cumberland, and obtaining the potent relic of St Cuthbert's banner from Durham to lead the Pilgrim army [25 *pp. 136–7, 146, 427–8*].

Barnard Castle (garrisoned by several of Bowes's relatives) easily yielded to them, and they spoiled Bishop Tunstall's palace at Bishop Auckland before sending off a major part of their force on 18 October to join Aske at York, retaining a central organization at Jervaulx Abbey [25 *p. 179*]. By 21 October they were beginning a week-long siege of Skipton Castle, trapping Henry Clifford, Earl of Cumberland and other refugee gentlemen who refused to join them [62 *pp. 84–7*].

The first musters in Westmorland were at Kirkby Stephen, on 16 October, probably in response to a summons from Richmond. The vicar of Brough, Robert Thompson, emerged as the local leader and soon companies were coming in from the surrounding villages to march westward to muster at Penrith in Cumberland. Here, on 19 October, four captains were appointed and took the names of Charity, Faith, Poverty and Pity. The rebels hoped to recruit the only city of their area, Carlisle, but the city authorities, perhaps influenced by the arrival of the fugitive Lord Clifford at Carlisle Castle, remained cool. The insurgent army ignored the Pontefract truce of late October and made repeated attempts to break the city's resistance by force until persuaded to a truce by Sir Christopher Dacre: the Dacre name could command respect where the widely unpopular Cliffords could not [25 *pp. 354–5*].

The chances of Pilgrim success in central and south Lancashire depended on the Earl of Derby. After rumours that he would join the rebellion, the king secured his loyalty by sending him a commission, giving him authority over a large area of Lancashire, Cheshire and North Wales, and after receiving this on 23 October, Derby took a firm lead against the rebels. Rather than sending a company to join Aske, Lancashire rebels concentrated their thousands of supporters on restoring the abbey of Sawley and containing the threat from Derby. Given Derby's attitude, it proved impossible to coerce Lancashire gentlemen into supporting the insurrection [55; 118 *p. 175*; 25 *pp. 231, 432*]. By contrast, the Dent rebels (the first oath-takers in all the north) had succeeded in recruiting local gentry to their cause, after extending their area of operations to the region round Kendal in north Lancashire. Now they marched south to take Lancaster on 28 October, in order to confront the earl [25 *pp. 253–4, 434*].

Altogether, by late October, nine well-armed 'hosts' had gathered and formed coherent organizations which had reduced opposition north of central Lancashire and the River Don to a few isolated outposts held by loyalist notables [25 *p. 3*]. The government was caught unawares; on 19 October the king had disbanded his large army that had gathered in the south at Ampthill to march on Lincolnshire, thinking that it was no longer needed. The Duke of Suffolk was too busy quietening Lincolnshire to cope with Yorkshire and the Earl of Shrewsbury still awaited the king's orders with his forces at Nottingham. For three weeks the rising was allowed to proceed unimpeded, but there was a hesitation in rebel strategy which in the long term gave the government its chance. Aske's intention throughout the campaign he directed was to overawe the government into granting the demands of the north, by presenting a show of force, while doing everything possible to avoid the use of force. Only one man was killed during the Pilgrimage, and that was an accident. Aske did not want to advance south unless Henry refused the Pilgrims' petition and he had no plan to form an alternative government or remove the king. Nevertheless, his aims to give the north a say in the affairs of the nation, to remove Cromwell and reverse the thrust of the Henrician Reformation could not possibly have been achieved without the exercise of massive force.

Aske knew that to make a decisive impact on Henry it was essential to have the backing of the great men of the north; by 19 October he knew also that much of the country beyond the Don was behind him. That day he appeared before Lord Darcy, Edward Lee, Archbishop of York, and forty or so knights and gentlemen who had taken refuge with Darcy at Pontefract Castle. Aske explained to them the Pilgrims' cause, boldly blaming them for not advising the king of the spread of heresy and the abuses of the monastic visitors. He argued, on practical grounds, that the abbeys should stand, maintaining that they were essential to the economy of the north [*Doc. 5*]. He told the archbishop he expected him to mediate for the Pilgrims. Two days later Darcy surrendered the castle.

The Pontefract gentry now joined in the discussions as to the strategy to be pursued against the approaching royal army. Darcy and Sir Robert Constable quickly became leaders among the rebels. Meanwhile the government's plans were falling into confusion. It welcomed a defensive strategic plan suggested by the Duke of Norfolk on 20 October: the armies which he and the Earl of Shrewsbury led should form a line on the River Trent to block the rebels' advance south. However, contradictory government orders to Shrewsbury had already sent the Earl (after some hesitations) marching further north towards the River Don and Pontefract; the defensive plan was wrecked. Norfolk, who had only just reached Newark-on-Trent from the south on 23 October, now had little option but to negotiate; the royal armies were dangerously far apart and vastly outnumbered by the Pilgrims. He sent a message to the Pilgrims by Lancaster Herald suggesting that bloodshed might be avoided if four of the Pilgrims met him at Doncaster to explain the causes of their rising. This letter was delivered to the rebel vanguard just to the south of Pontefract on 24 October [*25 pp. 374–86*].

There was disagreement among the Pilgrims as to whether they should treat with Norfolk. Their army of 30,000 was well disciplined and overwhelmingly strong beside the 8,000 men at the most that Shrewsbury had with him across the Don. But Aske argued that Norfolk, remembered and respected in the north as a hero of Flodden, might use his influence at Court on their behalf. He wanted to trust Norfolk and, with Darcy's backing, he won. Those who doubted Norfolk's intentions were more realistic, as before the meeting on Doncaster Bridge he wrote to Henry: 'I beseech you to take in gode part what so ever promes I shall make unto the rebells for sewerly I shall observe no part thereoff.'

The leaders decided to make their petition to Norfolk very general, leaving the maximum room for negotiation. Their five articles were in substance those drawn up before York; but instead of mentioning the Acts for the subsidy and the suppression and the Statute of Uses by name, they merely asked that 'unpopular statutes might be repealed' and 'the Faith truly maintained' [*35*] [*Doc. 3*]. Aske did not go to the bridge himself but ordered a general muster of the Pilgrims on the plain beyond it: they stood as a menacing background to the truce which was signed on 27 October. This first 'appointment' was the climax of the northern demonstration.

No full account of the 27 October meeting survives but, from a conversation between Darcy and Somerset Herald a few weeks later it appears that Norfolk did his utmost to bring the gentry to treachery. Lord Darcy indignantly refused:

> I had rather my hed stryken of [he told the herald], than I wold defyle my cote armor, for it shall never be sayd that old Thome shall have one treators tothe in his hed. . . . For my part I have byn and ever wylbe true both to kyng henry the vii and to the kyng our soverayn lord and I defye hym that wyll say the contrary, for as I have ever say one god one feth and one kyng.

But when it came to giving up his captain, whose cause was the unity of the commonwealth, he could not do it:

> For he that promysseth to be true to one, and deseyveth him, may be called a treator: whych shall never be seyd in me for what is a man but is promysse.

Here is the central dilemma of the Pilgrim leaders, a dilemma that faced Aske when in his examination he was asked how he could reconcile his duty of obedience to the king with the oath he swore on 4 October. It was a dilemma that neither Darcy, Aske, nor any of the Pilgrims, could solve.

Darcy had other good reasons to refuse to betray his captain on Doncaster Bridge. He had come to be afraid of his own men who, he told the herald, 'bycause wee tarried a whyll abowght the entreatie wold have ronned apon us to have kylled us sayng that we wold bytray them'. Yet even more he feared going to London. 'Hold up thy longe clee and promyse me that I shall have the Kynges favor and shalbe indeferently hard, and I wyll come to Dancastre to yow', he told Shrewsbury. 'Than ye shall not come it' the earl replied. Darcy knew he had committed himself too far.

The agreement reached on 27 October was that Sir Ralph Ellerker and Robert Bowes should carry the Pilgrims' petition to the king and a truce should be observed until they returned. Norfolk had failed to detach the gentry from the commons, so he compromised. He had no choice. It was 'not possible', he reported to the Council, 'to have yeven batayle but upon apparaunt los theroff'. He had 'no horsemen and they all the floure of the north' and most of his own soldiers 'thought and think their quarelles to be gode and godly'. But the bond between gentry and commons was still fragile. Beacons were left ready for firing to call to a new summons if necessary, just as the promise of further musters had been made in Lincolnshire. As in Lincolnshire, some murmured that the gentlemen would betray them as they waited the return of the negotiators.

Ellerker and Bowes reached Windsor on 2 November. The same day the king, in his own hand, wrote a reply to the rebel petition. It was a long justification of his rule, emphasizing his 'good discretion' in choosing councillors and reproving the Pilgrims for rising 'upon false reports and surmises'. One passage displays Henry's characteristic self-righteous indignation:

> What King hath kept you all his subjects so long in wealth and peace . . . so indifferently ministered justice to all, both high and low; so defended you all from outward enemies; so fortified the frontiers of this realm, to his no little and in a manner inestimable charges? And all for your wealths and sureties.

Finally he declared his intention through the 'pity and compassion' of 'our princely heart' to pardon all but ten ringleaders.

Henry thought that the rebellion would now collapse as it had done in Lincolnshire. His paramount concern was to claim victims and display his victory. He knew he could not afford to make concessions to this challenge as he had to the passive resistance of 1525. Nevertheless his blustering self-confidence was misplaced. Norfolk realized that the best policy was to temporize, so he persuaded the king to delay proclaiming his reply in the north, and make as many apparent concessions as possible. When Ellerker and Bowes laid the king's message before the chief captains of the Pilgrimage at Darcy's home at Templehurst on 18 November, it contained no reply to the articles but an offer of further negotiations between 300 of the Pilgrims, under safe conduct if they wished, and the Duke of Norfolk.

Henry's original reply had in fact been released and read at Skipton a few days before. It had increased the already extreme uneasiness of the truce. The movements of royal troops, particularly just south of the Humber, and rumours of a siege of Hull and a plot to capture Aske, alarmed the north throughout November. The delay in the return of Ellerker and Bowes was regarded with the utmost suspicion by the commons: 'the Lords and Gentlemen have noe such power as they had among them, they will not suffer two of them to talk together in private', reported Norfolk to the king [61 p. 75]. There were continual complaints on both sides of threatening moves and breaches of the truce.

On 21 November the council of the Pilgrims met at York and Robert Bowes gave the captains a detailed account of his visit to Windsor, assuring them that he was satisfied as to the king's good faith and mercy. In the discussions which followed one group, led by Sir Robert Constable, were moved by such violent hatred of Cromwell and such fear of his influence over the king that they wanted to 'have all the country made sure from the Trent northwards' and then 'condescend to a meeting'. The rest wanted conference. It was Constable who read to the council a letter, dated 10 November, from Cromwell to Sir Ralph Eure, who had stood siege through October at Scarborough. If the rebellion continued, Cromwell had said, it would be so crushed, that 'their example shall be fearful to all subjects whiles the world doth endure'. Despite this glimpse of the government's deviousness, the peace party's argument prevailed. Nothing, they maintained, could be lost by treating with Norfolk, whose influence it was hoped might rise as Cromwell's waned. Messages were sent to all the counties of the north summoning the Pilgrims' representatives to a second meeting or 'appointment' at Doncaster.

In his message to the rebels, discussed at York, Henry told them that he found their articles 'general, dark and obscure'. The purpose of the council held at Pontefract from 2 to 4 December was to clarify the issues which the Pilgrims should debate at Doncaster and to draw up a definitive statement of their programme. This twenty-four article manifesto was written out by Aske in consultation with Darcy. Each item was then approved by the Pilgrim captains. Aske was genuinely concerned to gather the views of all parts of the north. His notices of the Pontefract meeting brought in representatives from all the hosts of the northern counties. In the final document he was able to combine articles based on the petitions of the commons with the grievances of the gentry as expressed in the statements that several of them drew up. An assembly of north-country divines also sat concurrently with the council and made resolutions in sympathy with their programme. Aske regarded it as of the greatest importance that the Pilgrims should have the sanction of the church for their stand. Archbishop Lee was allowed to preach in the parish church on Sunday 3 December in the hope that he would support their cause. But when he told a crowded congregation of gentry and commons that the sword was given to none but a prince, the commons exploded in fury. Lee's rebuff was a nasty jolt to the rebels' confidence.

Until almost the last moment Henry insisted that Norfolk must except the ringleaders from the pardon; his final instructions (sent on 2 December) were that the duke should grant a general pardon, prolong the truce and promise a parliament wherever the rebels wished it. Norfolk received these orders just before the ten knights, ten esquires, and twenty commons appointed came to him at the White Friars in Doncaster on 6 December. Aske and his companions fell to their knees to beg the king's pardon and favour. Norfolk said that Henry would grant this, and a free parliament. This put him in a strong position when it came to discussing the articles. He was able to argue that most of the acts to which the Pilgrims objected could be considered at that parliament. He avoided committing himself as to when and where the parliament should be held. On one point the rebels were adamant: the suppressed abbeys should stand until their case had been brought before parliament again. Norfolk had no power to grant this but saw that it was essential if a settlement was to be reached. He compromised by insisting that the abbeys should make a formal surrender to the king's commissioners but that they should then be restored again by the king's authority until the parliament met.

The next morning Aske announced the terms for peace to the 3,000 commons waiting at Pontefract. He was back at Doncaster when he heard that they were not satisfied and were threatening to raise all Yorkshire again. He had to return to Pontefract to persuade them that all would be well. When Lancaster Herald had read the king's pardon on 8 December, the commons began to go home. The gentlemen meanwhile rode to Doncaster once more and there, in the presence of Norfolk, Aske knelt down and humbly asked the assembly that they should no longer call him captain. They agreed and the Pilgrims tore off their badges of the Five Wounds, saying 'We will all wear no badge nor sign but the badge of our sovereign lord'.

Aske thought he had won. Everyone in the north expected Norfolk's speedy return with the king's confirmation of the terms agreed. But for several weeks nothing happened. The king neither ratified nor repudiated the terms that had been made. His policy throughout had been marked by vacillation and inconsistency but now he could await the excuse to exact his revenge and vindicate the honour of his house in bloodshed. The terms had never been written down and Henry no more intended to keep his own promise of a general pardon than Norfolk's that the suppression should be reversed. In London it was rumoured that the rebels had submitted to mercy and the king, his new queen and the Court celebrated Christmas with lavishness and splendour. In fact Henry had won [113 *pp. 341–6*].

## THE CAUSES OF THE REBELLION

The causes of the Lincolnshire rising and the Pilgrimage of Grace have become highly controversial. One crucial question at issue is whose risings they were. The rebellions have commonly been seen as an authentic expression of the grievances of the north as a whole, a massive popular indictment of the Henrician regime. They have also sometimes been viewed as a feudal or neo-feudal phenomenon, a reaction by the old-established and overmighty families of the north to Tudor centralization. A deliberately provocative reinterpretation was that of Sir Geoffrey Elton: 'in the main the northern risings represent the effort of a defeated Court faction to create a power base in the country for the purpose of achieving a political victory at Court' [48 *p. 212*]. Equally controversial is the debate over the real motivation of those involved: were the central grievances really about religion, or primarily economic and social?

Margaret and Ruth Dodds, who first told the full story of the Pilgrimage in an exciting and dependable narrative, undoubtedly took the evidence presented by men implicated in the rising too much at face value [44]. Aske was bound to paint the Pilgrimage as a popular movement that he was powerless to halt, in order to exculpate himself. Additionally, the Dodds introduced a misleading division in their analysis, trying to distinguish between a religious movement directed by gentlemen and a social movement directed against gentlemen. Thomas Cromwell may also have contributed his own misleading gloss in the aftermath of the rebellion. Loth to make serious concessions on the official policy of religious change which he was sponsoring, he may have emphasized the agrarian grievances in certain areas of rebellion because he was more prepared to meet local concerns on those issues. Distortions such as these have led commentators to make false distinctions between the primary motivations in different components of the risings [25 *pp. 186, 277*].

How far then was the Pilgrimage authentic? – how far, that is, do the protests that appear in the rebel articles represent the genuine grievances of those who left their homes as winter was approaching in order to march to Pontefract? In certain cases there is little cause for doubt. Recent taxation was much disliked and the new subsidy, uniquely, had come in peacetime. Some historians have seen the 1534 Subsidy Act as an attempt at fiscal revolution, because it justified parliamentary taxation primarily in terms of the civil benefits conferred on the realm by the king's government [63; 87 *pp. 5–6, 46, 82–3*]. This point was not missed in the north. When

Holland rose to support the rest of Lincolnshire, the articles there stated that the king should demand no more money of his subjects except for the defence of the realm. Coming after two years of dearth, following bad weather and poor harvests, resentment at the new subsidy may have been particularly important in prompting support for the rising in the Yorkshire dales and in Marshland: the evidence of the tax assessments in the early Tudor period has shown that these were the poorest areas of the West Riding.

The final manifesto at Pontefract contained two articles relating strictly to economic matters. Enclosure was almost certainly the less important of the two. It was only a grievance in the valley communities of the West Riding, in Lake County uplands and in certain densely populated areas such as the vale of York, Furness, the Eden Valley and parts of the Cumberland coast [102 *pp. 49, 80; 57 pp. 60–6*]. Entry fines (that is, payment on taking up a tenancy by inheritance or sale, and locally known as gressums) were a far more serious matter of complaint west of the Pennines than enclosures. The Westmorland commons mentioned other economic grievances, not taken up by Aske, in their letter to Lord Darcy. Their complaint about tithes, and attacks on tithe-barns, were not an assault on the Church, but rather an element in the bitterness against unpopular landlords (usually in this case absentees, and represented by lay agents) – an attempt to modify a system which both laymen and clerics had corrupted [*57 pp. 47–60; 25 p. 173*].

The hardest problem, in relation to the question of authenticity, is how far the Pilgrimage was a spontaneous or popular religious rising. Certain articles at Pontefract can be attributed with no great difficulty to clerical pressure. Attacks on benefit of clergy and the privileges of sanctuary, the recent abolition of the liberties of Beverley, Durham, Ripon and St Peter of York, were predictably resented among the clergy themselves. But the religious attitudes of the mass of the laity are more difficult to determine. Their allegiance may have owed something to cleverly mounted propaganda designed to present official religious change as endangering the whole fabric of religious life. It was, after all, quite plausible to represent what was happening as a threat to parish life, which was what would concern most people. If monasteries were dissolved, what did that mean for parish churches which were appropriated to them, and which in some cases were part of the monastery church building? Traditional rituals, practices and beliefs appeared to be threatened. In the East Riding the people grumbled that they were no longer allowed to keep St Wilfrid's day. At Kirkby Stephen there was fury when the priest failed to bid St Luke's day; at Kendal on the Sunday after Christmas some of the rebels 'stirred up suddenly at bedes bidding and would have had the priest bid the bedes the old way and pray for the Pope'. A month later they forced the curate to observe the time-honoured way of prayer. 'Fundamentally', Penry Williams has written, 'the Pilgrims were protesting against an unprecedented intrusion by the Crown into their local communities and traditional ways' [136 p. 321].

Scott Harrison and Michael Bush have both suggested that the rebels in the Lake Counties were far more concerned with religious grievances than has been previously acknowledged. The risings there were characterized by ritual processions, and there were the same rumours about confiscation of church jewels and taxes on christenings, marriages and burials as were common elsewhere [57 p. 72; 25 pp. 372–3]. From the earliest outbreaks in September, in the lordship of Dent, one of the most striking characteristics of the rebellion was its insistence on the swearing of oaths. The example had been set by the national campaign of oath-swearing to the new royal succession in 1534. Now the oaths were to wider concepts than simply dynastic succession: holy Church, the commonwealth, as well as the preservation of the king's person [Doc. 4]. Aske's achievement in building on all this to create a demonstration that had an atmosphere of honour and chivalry was remarkable. For a few weeks his vision and purposefulness gave the movement an almost mystical aura. However, even before his intervention, the most constructive act of the rebels was a religious one: to affirm the place of monastic life in their own communities, by restoring dissolved religious houses.

Perhaps sixteen of the fifty-five monasteries that had been dissolved under the Act of Suppression, passed in March 1536, were restored by the Pilgrims. It is hard to determine the initiative behind these restorations. There is good evidence for popular support for the restoration of Cartmel, Conishead and Sawley: in fact all four suppressed in Cumbria were re-opened, in areas remote from Aske's initiative and before the hosts had publicly made contact [55]. William Hungate, the farmer of Nunburnholme in Yorkshire, held the local inhabitants responsible there as well. Aske maintained that St Clement's Priory in York was restored 'because the commons would needs put them in' but he certainly organized it himself. Elsewhere parish priests, monks and friars probably played a leading part. For Aske, the essence of the rising was that it was a spiritual protest by the laity on behalf of the Church. From the time that he entered York, he exalted the cause of the monasteries into the rallying cry of the movement: it was summarized for most of the participants by the intensely emotional symbol of the badge of the Five Wounds of Christ.

The case for the monasteries that Aske put forward so ably under examination probably includes most of the motives which made the abbeys (as Norfolk wrote in 1537) 'greatlie beloved with the people' [*Doc. 11*]. It is interesting to compare this with the much less sentimental case Aske argued to the lords at Pontefract [*Doc. 5*]. He then emphasized the social and economic role of the monasteries. There is no doubt that the day-to-day gifts of food and clothing and hospitality to northern travellers that the houses in the Pennines offered made them valuable to the community as a whole [*57 p. 12*]. Their importance to the laity was by no means limited to the 3 per cent of their income allowable in the *Valor Ecclesiasticus* as charity [*76 p. 264*]. It was the usefulness of the abbeys to the gentry and substantial tenantry that Aske was particularly concerned to emphasize to his Pontefract audience. They acted as the focal point of the social life of a neighbourhood: abbeys provided some rudimentary education, safe deposit for valuable documents, tenancies for farmers, and a place to dispose of unmarried daughters or, through the system of corrodies, aged relations. Aske persuasively maintained that not only would all these services be lost, but that the future economic effects of the appropriation by southern landowners of northern monastic lands would be disastrous. Though exaggerated, his argument that shortage of coin could drive the north into either rebellion or treaty with the Scots was probably not without foundation [*55 pp. 53–60*].

Aske saw the religious role of the monasteries as twofold: they maintained by their 'gostly liffing' an exalted ideal that was to him an essential element of the Christian tradition and they provided 'speritual informacion, and preching' to a people 'not well taught the law of God'. The extent to which the monastic ideal was in fact being realized at the dissolution has been argued over at length by historians. Professor Knowles has provided a comprehensive and balanced survey of the evidence and dealt with the grosser allegations of the monastic visitors [*76*]. How did people other than Aske himself regard the monasteries in 1536? The Pilgrims' ballad makes it evident that the commons did not make a distinction between religious and economic usefulness [*Doc. 6*]. They simply identified the threat to the Church with the threat to the poor. In the same way an anonymous petitioner to Aske linked the relief of poverty and 'the prayer for the founders and service of God maintained' [35 *p. 67*].

What should we make of the involvement of the north's great families? Henry Percy, sixth Percy Earl of Northumberland, was a crucial figure in the crisis of the 1530s in northern England, though his behaviour during the actual rising was ambivalent. The Percies' extensive estates in Northumberland, Yorkshire and Cumberland made them the most powerful family in the north, despite the blow to their power and prestige represented by the lynching of the fourth Percy Earl in 1489 (see Chapter 3 above). By the 1530s the sixth earl had rebuilt what seemed an impregnable hold on the area, through his wardenship of the east and middle marches and his lieutenancy in Yorkshire. He was also sheriff of Northumberland for life. But his position in relation to the crown was in fact perilous. He was regarded with the deepest suspicion in London because of his northern prestige. A precontract of marriage with Anne Boleyn made him insecure when the divorce became an issue; in his last years he was certainly in poor health, and perhaps even mentally unstable. In 1535 he made approaches to Chapuys; throughout the previous decade he had tried to fortify his position in the north by the multiplication of offices and fees. He was estranged from his wife and had no heir; he was also on bad terms with his brother, Sir Thomas, to whom Henry in any case objected as his heir in 1535. This is the background to Northumberland's eccentric and sensational gesture of 1536: he made the king his sole heir. This was his means of escape from the appalling dilemma of the great magnate faced with a suspicious master [118 *pp. 171–2*; 62 *p. 79*].

After this it was impossible for Northumberland to emerge as a leader of the Pilgrims. Publicly he remained aloof throughout the rising; in fact he passively accepted it, surrendering Wressle Castle to Aske and recognizing him as 'captain of the baronage'. While the earl was still in London in early October the commons had shouted 'thousands for a Percy' at the castle gate; elsewhere in the north his family quickly became leaders. Sir Ingram Percy, constable of Alnwick Castle, swore Northumberland people to the Pilgrims' cause. Sir Thomas, who marched to York with 5,000 men from east Yorkshire, was referred to as 'the lock, key and wards of this matter'. When he entered York the commons 'showed such affection towards him as they showed towards none other. Gorgeously he rode through the city in complete harness with feathers trimmed as well as he might deck himself at that time.' Not surprisingly, a significant number of leading Yorkshire gentry brought into leadership roles in the rebellion turn out to be Percy tenants. Four were actually members of Northumberland's council: Aske was his legal adviser, Sir Robert Constable was lord of Flamborough and thirty-six other manors, and Robert Lascelles and William Stapulton were holders of important Percy estates. Even so, M.L. Bush's detailed examination of the various hosts concluded that even the army from the heartland of Percy estates in east Yorkshire was primarily 'a movement of the commons'. None of the nine hosts was in fact organized in a feudal manner: their organization was generally done on a parish basis [25 p. 210].

In other respects, the Pilgrimage is unconvincing as a neo-feudal rising. The Earl of Derby, as we have seen, became an aggressive champion of the king. The traditional magnate of the north-west, Lord Dacre, was first besieged by the rebels at Naworth and later kept so far out of the conflict as to disappear temporarily from the records. The Earl of Westmorland was captured by the rebels in his castle, and in the years after the Pilgrimage he remained deeply traumatized by the disloyalty of his household and tenants [61 pp. 63–4, 70–1]. Similarly, the Clifford Earl of Cumberland found himself deserted by his gentry retinue when the rebellion broke out and besieged in Skipton Castle. Some historians have exaggerated and misunderstood the evidence for the Cliffords' relations with their tenants. It was said that after the Pilgrimage 'no man was worse beloved' in the north-west than Cumberland, but that may well have been a retrospective reflection of resentment at his refusal to join his tenants in support of the risings. If the Cliffords were indeed unpopular with their fellow-notables, it was because they had threatened the balance of power in the north by their dynastic good fortune: the earl's son married the king's niece in 1535 [62 pp. 74, 78, 90–1; 25 p. 155]. Apart from Lord Darcy at Pontefract, the peers who gave more or less equivocal support to the rebels were lesser figures: Barons Lumley, Latimer, Scrope of Bolton and Conyers. Moreover, there was nothing feudal about the Pilgrims' oath [Doc. 4].

Prominent landed families did not even stand together. Lord Darcy's two sons failed to take up their father's cause. Robert Aske's brother defended Skipton for the Earl of Cumberland. The Duke of Norfolk commented upon the familial divisions that came into the open when the die was cast: 'Fie, fie upon the Lord Darcy,' he declared, 'the most arrant traitor that ever was living and yet both his sons true knights; old Sir Robert Constable as ill as he is and all his blood true men.' Likewise, it is difficult to accept M.E.

James's picture of a united Lincolnshire gentry community rising in opposition to Court policy, embodied by the Duke of Suffolk, whom they resented as a new force in county politics imposed on them from outside. Suffolk in fact had very little to do with the county until after the collapse of the 1536–37 commotions [68; 52 *p. 56*].

Professor Elton's revisionist interpretation of the risings had as its avowed agenda the reassertion of political history's importance over economic and social history. By 'political', Elton meant politics at a national level, so his account implicitly also condemned localist interpretations, and any political analysis which took popular politics seriously. This produced some strange results. One of his chief supposed proofs for 'upper-class' leadership was that rebellion was spread by 'wild rumours and stories', yet characteristically in early modern Europe countrywide rumours are the stuff of mass politics, not of aristocratic intrigue. Nor could Elton bring himself to believe that ordinary people were capable of the planning which he acknowledged must lie behind the rapid outbreaks of trouble, despite repeated evidence to the contrary in Tudor England [48 *pp. 193–4*]. His general interpretation can hardly stand. Particularly, thanks to the new primary source evidence provided by Richard Hoyle [61], it is clear that the initiative lay with popular unrest, and that the shape of the rising, particularly in Lincolnshire, caught off-guard even those gentry who became deeply involved. The continued mistrust between the crowds and the gentry leadership which they had coopted is equally unmistakeable.

Given this mistrust, why did the commons insist so repeatedly on gentry and noble families assuming leadership roles? M.L. Bush plausibly explains their behaviour as a reflection of their belief in a 'society of orders', nobility, commons and clergy: all the nine main hosts tried to recruit noble leaders because they felt that gentry ought to lead them, and most of the hosts succeeded. Some of these leaders were purely symbolic representatives of ancient families who because of their youth could hardly act as practical military figures: the thirteen-year-old Lord Neville or the nineteen-year-old George Bowes, for instance [25 *pp. 64, 75, 158*]. Equally significant is the way in which the hosts generally did not allow the clergy to take an active fighting role in their armies; they were relegated either to providing funds, or to taking appropriate symbolic roles as leaders of processions or chaplains. Each order had its characteristic and particular role to play.

Many leading gentry became leaders of the hosts because they saw it as a form of damage limitation: as local magistrates, they had a duty to maintain order, and in the face of huge demonstrations and no means of coercion at their disposal, this was the only route left to them. There was good reason for them to fear popular violence, at least against property if not against life. S.J. Gunn makes a significant connection between the actions of prominent Lincolnshire gentry in 1536 and the memories which several of them would have of military commands in the generally dismal English campaigns of the 1510s and 1520s in France. There they frequently faced army mutinies. 'When common soldiers mutinied, they could be neither ignored nor left to their own devices. Some semblance of order had to be maintained, if necessary by a partial or total concession of the mutineers' demands, while the king's instructions, and pardon for any departure from orders, were obtained as a matter of urgency' [52 p. 70]. This looks very like what happened in the Lincolnshire rising, and eventually also in Yorkshire.

Equally important to note is what M.L. Bush terms 'an aristocratic conspiracy of inaction'. It is likely that many leading gentry could have done much to stem the tide of popular disaffection by taking a decisive stand against it, as in fact they had done successfully against Yorkshire agrarian unrest in the previous year. Instead, strongly disapproving of a range of government initiatives in legal and religious change, they stood aside and allowed events to develop. Only when Pontefract Castle was forced to yield did the leading figures of Yorkshire, who had taken refuge there, find it impossible to maintain this stance of benevolent neutrality; the commons made it clear that now they must become positively involved [25 pp. 131–3, 408].

Elton did raise questions which should warn us against taking any one simple explanation of the risings. He drew attention to those he saw as key figures: Aske himself, Lord Darcy and Lord Hussey. Aske's story of how he was forced to join the rebels makes no sense at all. In fact his confessions, taken as a whole, a brilliant exercise in special pleading, have probably done more than anything else to confuse historians about the actual nature of the rebellion. Darcy, as we have seen, pretended at first that he was opposed to the rising. By 1 October he had his extensive following of knights, esquires and gentlemen ready 'to serve the King's grace' upon an hour's warning. Yet he surrendered Pontefract quite extraordinarily quickly. Moreover, when he did so he was ready to distribute to the rebels numerous badges of the Five Wounds of Christ, badges which had presumably been stored in his castle since his retinue wore them on an expedition against the Moors in Spain more than twenty years before. None of these men, Professor Elton argued, can seriously be thought to have been taken entirely by surprise in October 1536. But can we see this as a decisive argument that their political disaffection lay at the heart of the rising?

From around 1530 to 1535 Darcy and Hussey were prominent members of the 'Aragonese' faction at Court which had supported Queen Catherine of Aragon and her daughter Mary, and opposed the king's campaign to replace Catherine by Anne Boleyn. Hussey indeed was Mary's chamberlain. In 1534 it seems that Hussey and Darcy seriously contemplated a resort to arms: in a conversation with Chapuys, Darcy spoke of organizing an insurrection of the people and subsequently bringing in the nobility and clergy. Although Darcy returned to Yorkshire in 1535, in London, new prospects opened up for the 'Aragonese' grouping. With Catherine's death in January 1536, Henry was in their eyes free to marry again, and then the Boleyn marriage collapsed and Anne was executed. However, Hussey's hopes of restoring the succession to Princess Mary were thwarted by the machinations of Thomas Cromwell, who proved the real winner in the disgrace of the Boleyns. Hussey lost his office in Mary's household and his wife was imprisoned in the Tower, after he was alleged to have encouraged the Princess to resist Cromwell's demands that she fully accept the royal supremacy.

Besides the commons of the north, plenty of northern gentry were also grieved at the policies of the Cromwellian regime. No one made this discontent more explicit than Sir Thomas Tempest, who asserted in a paper that he sent to the Pilgrims at Pontefract that Cromwell had turned parliament into a mere puppet of the king's chief minister. Tempest provided a thoughtful and forthright exposition of the responsibilities of kingship that neither Cromwell nor the king would have found agreeable reading. Thus it is possible to see one element of the rebellion as a last-ditch attempt by those who were out of favour at Court to restore their political fortunes by seizing on the discontents and puzzlements of others. These men sought to promote a cause – the restoration of Mary – in which they sincerely believed. The intention, according to this interpretation, was 'to create a power base in the country for the purpose of achieving a political victory at Court' [47 *pp. 260–71*; 48 *pp. 211–14*].

Elton's focus on central politics also makes sense of many articles in the Pontefract manifesto which historians have found most puzzling. Thus the Second Succession Act makes its appearance among the articles because this, for Aragonese politicians, was the crux of the matter. The clause about Scotland in the article relating to the Succession can be attributed to Aske himself: he was concerned that unless it was definitely established that Mary should succeed, the king might look seriously at the Scottish claim through his sister Margaret. Aske was determined that 'if the crown were given by the King's highness to an alien . . . it is a void gift, because he is not born under the allegiance of this crown'. The attack on Cromwell, Audley and Rich was for the commons probably no more than a search for scapegoats, but for those with an eye on high politics in London, it can be seen as a deadly serious campaign against a rival faction. The 1534 Treason Act, the royal supremacy and the spread of heresy were given close attention by Darcy and Aske because they were the obvious manifestations of Cromwell's rule.

The supremacy article was confessedly included on Aske's initiative and little interest was shown in it even by the other leaders. Aske, perhaps alone, saw an overriding principle at stake, a principle which he was ready to state under interrogation: the supremacy 'could not stand with Goddes law'. His claim that it was 'in al menz mouthes that the Supremacy should sound to be a measure of a division from the unite of catholyke church' is almost certainly exaggerated. The rebel lists of heresies and heretics suggest confusion and uncertainty, even among the gentry at the head of the rising, about exactly which representatives of religious change to denounce. The York list lumps together Protestants like Bishop Nicholas Shaxton of Salisbury with the orthodox Bishop Longland of Lincoln whose administration had alienated many in his diocese. At Pontefract, continental reformers like Oecolampadius and Bucer, very little of whose works had been translated into English and certainly not under their own name, were mentioned together with Wycliffe, Tyndale and Barnes.

We are left, when the articles so far discussed are set aside, with a medley of demands that can be attributed to one or other group or individual among the northern gentry implicated in the rising. A complaint about the Statute of Uses was taken over from the first set of articles formulated by some of the Lincolnshire gentry led by George Stones. He had encountered some difficulty in getting the countrymen to understand why this statute was something that the country should resist. The professional grievances of the lawyers of the north, ably represented by Aske himself, appear in such pronouncements as the call for a ban on summoning people on subpoena from beyond the Trent and the attack on certain practices of the escheators. The Pilgrims' manifestos were highly eclectic documents.

Nevertheless, there are clear weaknesses in Elton's account even of the national political dimension. Hussey's and Darcy's conversations with Chapuys in 1534 may be only marginally relevant: there was always talk in Chapuys's lodgings of risings and foreign invasions, but nothing came of it before 1536, and there is no evidence that Chapuys was involved in the events of this year to any degree [61 *p. 79n*]. More seriously, Elton relied too much on M.E. James's account of Hussey's centrality to rebellion in 1536: Hussey was a very elderly politician whose importance was in decline not just nationally but locally, and his main contribution to events seems to have been to stay on the sidelines and dither too long [52 *p. 54*]. His execution in 1537 is not a clear demonstration of his subversive role in 1536.

The safest conclusion about the stirs of 1536 is that several disparate social groupings and concerns came together because of disparate provocations, and pooled their grievances in the lists of demands which survive. The first outbreaks of open protest look as if they were planned, but the planning does not seem to come from the ranks of national politicians; rather leadership was initially from yeomen, skilled craftsmen and the lower clergy, given their opportunity by the nobility's 'conspiracy of inaction'. Their grievances were fears for their religion, their community life and their prosperity. When the northern gentry and nobility cooperated it was in order to contain and channel the anger as best they could. The one clear exception is Robert Aske: in any case not a county gentleman, but a curiously marginal figure in Yorkshire society, a man who because of his London links could mediate between centre and locality outside the normal communication channels of early Tudor government. He channelled this ability into a direct challenge to all aspects of government policy.

Given this combination of protest from a wide geographical and social spectrum of northern society, it is easy to see why the Pilgrimage could have been fatal for Henry's government: it came perilously close to succeeding, and was 'the largest popular revolt in English history' [36 *p. 63*]. If more leading noblemen of the north had backed it, all would have been lost for the evangelical clique around Cromwell in London. This was easily the most dangerous of all the unsuccessful rebellions of the Tudor period. Yet in the end, not enough of the north's natural leaders were prepared openly to support the movement: they were probably frightened by the fact that too many leaders had emerged from outside their charmed circle, and by the very provisional nature of the deference which they discovered in the lower orders. With many of those gentry and noblemen who did assume leadership roles using their position to slow the momentum of the rebel crowds, the Westminster government was given its chance to play for time and take the initiative. As C.S.L. Davies suggests, 'the end result of the Pilgrimage may have been to sow such distrust between clergy and commons, and between gentry and commons, as to prevent any repetition for a generation' [36 *p. 85*].

## HENRY VIII AND THE NORTH, 1537–47

After the negotiations at Doncaster the king's policy was to divide the gentry from the commons, and harry the north with propaganda on the sinfulness of rebellion. He was waiting his chance for revenge. This was provided by a rising in the East Riding on 16 January, a symptom of a widespread feeling of bewilderment and betrayal among the commons at the lack of action following the lavish royal promises. A mark of its separateness from the previous gentry leadership of the Pilgrimage was that its captain was not a Catholic but an enthusiast for the evangelical 'new learning': Sir Francis Bigod. Aske, at this time, was telling the northern gentry of the promises he had been given in London of a parliament in the north and a visit by the king. Bigod alone perceived the hollowness of the government's pardon. He evolved, with the yeoman Pilgrim captain John Hallom, a plan to capture Hull and Scarborough. If Norfolk came north he could be taken and used as an intermediary with the government. Professor Dickens regarded Bigod's scheme as 'the most interesting politico-military concept evolved by a Tudor rebel' [37 *p. 97*].

The outcome was pathetic and disastrous. Bigod had failed to make the minimum of contacts necessary among the local gentry. The few hundred commons who mustered briefly, held Beverley, after failing to capture Hull or Scarborough. Within a few days Bigod was a hunted fugitive. He was captured in Cumberland on 10 February. Here in February the commons mustered on their own initiative because their patience with the gentry had finally run out. They were routed in an attack on Carlisle.

These two outbursts of disorder gave Henry the excuse he needed to pursue a systematic policy of punishment. The Duke of Norfolk declared martial law in the West March, and rebels were hanged at

Carlisle and in the Cumberland villages [57 *pp. 119–26*]. During the spring, the gentry leaders were gradually rounded up, brought to London and tried. A total of 178 executions is recorded [46 *pp. 387–9*]. Among the gentry who were executed were Sir Thomas Percy, Sir Stephen Hammerton and Sir Francis Bigod. Lord Hussey was executed on 29 June, Lord Darcy was beheaded the following day. And on 12 July Robert Aske was drawn to his execution on Clifford's Tower at York. On the scaffold he made a confession characteristic of Henrician subjects about to die for treason: 'The King's Majesty, he said, he had greatly offended in breaking his laws whereunto every true subject is bounden by the commandment of God.'

In May 1537 Northumberland, unhappy under the shadow of treason, made over all his lands unconditionally to the crown. With his death in July, Henry had achieved the object for which he had been striving: the destruction of the Percy interest. But it might have been inferred from the Duke of Norfolk's harping on the need to have 'men of estimation and nobility' to rule the Marches that he too had ambitions to be an overmighty subject. Rather than take any such risk, Henry now accelerated his policy of building up a royal interest in the north, by giving increased authority to gentry families who had served him loyally. 'If it shall please his majesty', wrote the Council to Norfolk, 'to appoynt the meanest man to rule and govern in that place, is not his Graces authoritie sufficient to cause al men to serve his Grace under him without respect of the verie estate of the personage.' Henry added a note to this himself: 'For surely we woll not be bound of anecessitie to be served with lordes. But we woll be served with such men what degree soever as we shall appoint to the same.' In the appointment of Sir Thomas Wharton to the Wardenry of the West March in 1544 we can see Richard Morison's arguments for the claims of virtue above rank being put into practice [*Doc. 10*]. Wharton's qualification was that the king trusted him and he was an able administrator. He had already obtained the substance of the Warden's authority in 1537, thus curtailing the power of the Earl of Cumberland in the wake of the Earl's less-than-triumphant actions during the Pilgrimage [65].

In 1537 also the Council of the North was reorganized and put on a permanent footing [108, 18]. Many of the Pilgrim leaders, men like Sir Thomas Tempest, Sir Ralph Ellerker and Robert Bowes, were among its first members. Thus, through the new Council and the rule of men like Sir Thomas Wharton, the Henrician government tried to counteract the endemic violence and lawlessness of the north. Bowes and Ellerker, in a survey of the borders made in 1542, wrote that the borderers 'most prayses and cheryshes suche as begynne sonest in youthe to practise themselves in theftes and robberies contrary to the kinges graces lawes'. In the first decade of its existence the new Council not only had to cope with the persistent border feuds, but with the widespread discontent and antagonism to the regime which simmered in the years following the Pilgrimage [37]. The north's faith in the Percies did not die. While the substance of their power had passed to the king, numerous prophecies circulated foretelling the reawakening of their prestige: 'The moon shall kindle again, and take light of the sun, meaning by the moon the blood of the Percies.' The belief in their return to power was seen in almost magical terms. If anything happened to the king, a Yorkshire tiler told some friends in Kent in 1538, a Percy would inherit and 'he would cause England to shyne as bryght as seynt George' [46 *pp. 61–4*; 126 *pp. 400–1*].

Throughout 1537 popular sedition was always near the surface. In March Dr Dakyn, the vicar-general of the diocese of York, told the Privy Council that since the rising he had exhorted the people of Richmond to accept the royal supremacy only at the risk of his life. The Duke of Norfolk found it necessary to attend the suppression of Bridlington and Jervaulx in person because the neighbouring country was populous and the houses were 'greatly beloved'. Then in 1541 a new plot emerged, led by a small group of gentry and clergy in the Wakefield district. The plan was to kill the evangelical cleric Robert Holgate, the President of the Council of the North, and hold Pontefract Castle till help came from Scotland. The plot was caused by resentment at the punishments following the 1536 rising and the government's continuance of policies obnoxious to the north. The drive against the great abbeys and the seigneurial franchises in the years 1537–41 meant that by 1541 Aske's fears that the north would be drained of currency were being at least partially realized [*Doc. 5*]. Fifty to a hundred people seem to have been involved in the plot, of whom about fifteen were executed. There is little evidence that it engaged popular feeling on any scale [118 *p. 210*].

The swift discovery and crushing of the Wakefield plot demonstrated the utility of the new Council of the North. Yet, coinciding with new Scottish border raids, it caused Henry serious concern. He started to adopt a more friendly attitude to France. He took measures to strengthen the border towns against the Scots. Then, in the summer, at last he made a lavish progress to the north, hoping to overawe it with his royal person [102 *p. 50*; 113 *pp. 427–8*]. The government also took care not to push northern sensibilities too far: as major chantry colleges were dissolved in the south and west of England during Henry's last years, it was noticeable that no such colleges were dissolved in the north [34 *p. 61*].

This combination of personal attention and absence of further government provocation seems to have worked. For the last six years of Henry's reign there were no further plots and no cases of treason, and the north failed to rise for the old religion alongside the West Country in 1549. Temporarily at least, the north was tamed. But the absence of internal unrest in this period is only one side of the picture. The experiment of choosing wardens not from the nobility but from old border gentry, for example Sir Thomas Wharton and William Eure, was a failure. Since both had difficulties in securing military cooperation from the English borderers, the Henrician government was driven to rely increasingly during the 1540s on paid garrisons and foreign mercenaries to defend its northern frontier. The far north remained a pressing military and administrative problem.

# 5 THE WESTERN REBELLION

RIOT AND REBELLION IN THE WEST, 1547-49

The first insurrections of Cornishmen against the Edwardian Reformation, in 1547 and 1548, sprang from fear of the loss of church goods and the intense unpopularity of the government's agent, William Body. Body was an unscrupulous and avaricious careerist. He had obtained the archdeaconry of Cornwall in 1537 from Thomas Winter, Wolsey's illegitimate son, who was in debt to him. The Bishop of Exeter challenged Winter's right to transfer the archdeaconry to Body for a term of thirty-five years, and in 1541 the bishop's agents tried to prevent his collection of the clergy's procurations at Launceston. Body replied by a writ of praemunire against the bishop's official which was successful.

When Body returned to the county in 1547 and summoned the clergy to hear the Edwardian injunctions, he met with a hostile demonstration at Penryn that thoroughly alarmed the authorities. The college of St Mary and St Thomas at Glasney just outside Penryn was the largest religious foundation remaining in the county, with a revenue of £221 a year. The commissioners who were surveying the chantries were taking inventories of church goods, and it seems that Body gave the impression that the goods would be confiscated. The government dealt mildly with the disturbance on this occasion, and showed themselves anxious to appease the commons.

The next year Body was back in Cornwall visiting parish churches to ensure that the government's orders on the destruction of all images were being carried out. When Body arrived at Helston on 6 April, a mob, led by Martin Geoffrey, the priest of St Keverne (a repeatedly rebellious parish), set upon him and killed him. The Cornishmen had demonstrated their readiness to take the law into their own hands against an official they disliked and with whom they identified the new religious policy. The murder of Body was the first violent expression of their hostility to Protestant demolition of traditional rituals. John Resseigh, the yeoman leader of the mob, took his stand on the 'laws and ordinances touching the Christian religion' as they existed at the death of Henry VIII 'of blessed memory'. He challenged the right of a Protector to alter these laws. This could only be done by the king when he had come of age which, so far as Resseigh was concerned, was when he was twenty-four. That was thirteen years away. Meanwhile, Resseigh proclaimed defiantly in Helston market place, 'whosoever dare defend this Body and follow such new fashions as he did, we will punish him likewise'.

Such was the temper of the commons that the JPs cancelled the sessions to be held at Helston and arranged for those of the ringleaders whom they had managed to arrest to be tried at Launceston. The gentry had no hold over the far west and called on Sir Richard Edgecombe, one of the principal Devon gentry, to come to their aid. He collected people from the parishes in the east of the county on his way. But the victimization of Body had, for the moment satisfied the commons. The trouble died down and people returned to their homes. The government issued a general pardon, excepting twenty-eight of the ringleaders. Only ten of these were in fact hanged [*73 pp. 439–40*].

During the next year the religious policies initiated by Protector Somerset continued to make their impact on the county. The government made some attempt to be constructive: when the chantries were dissolved, arrangements were made for the continuance of four schools and four curacies in the larger parishes. A preacher was sent to begin the conversion of the county. But the atmosphere remained unsettled and even the boys of Bodmin school divided themselves into two factions, those who supported the old religion and those who supported the new. Their escapades led to their blowing up a calf and all being beaten.

It was the announcement of the new liturgy in the Prayer Book, to be uniformly used on Whitsunday 1549, that turned the Cornish opposition into full-scale rebellion. The commons from the villages around Bodmin persuaded Humphrey Arundell, a man with extensive estates in that area, to be their leader. He was clearly a troublemaker since he had appeared in a number of Chancery cases charged, among other things, with forcible entry upon other people's lands. The only other gentleman involved was John Winslade of Tregarrick. The rebels collected at Bodmin where they formed a camp. The articles drawn up there were very likely the work of the small group of priests, whose influence held the rebels together and with Arundell's organization gave the rising a defined purpose. Early in June the rebels advanced into Devon, leaving a small force to besiege Plymouth.

In Devon a rising began independently and spontaneously at Sampford Courtenay. Here, the priest, following the orders of the government, said the new service on Whitsunday, 10 June. But the next day the villagers persuaded him to defy the government. John Hooker, who wrote the only detailed contemporary account of the rebellion, recounts that he 'yielded to their wills and forthwith raversheth himself in his old popish attire and sayeth mass and all such services as in times past accustomed'. The Devonshire JPs lacked the confidence to impose the government's will; they could do nothing to prevent such outrages as the murder of one of the gentry who urged the people to remain peaceful and obedient. The Sampford Courtenay group and others from villages around joined the Cornishmen at Crediton, where a considerable force had gathered by 20 June.

News of the rebellion brought the Devonian knight Sir Peter Carew hastening back from his wife's estates in Lincolnshire. It is not certain whether Carew was acting on the government's orders or on his own initiative. He had served Henry VIII at Court and in France, had sat as MP for Tavistock in 1545 and had been sheriff of Devon in 1547. But he was a known evangelical and a most unsuitable choice to deal with a rebellion that was founded on religious conservatism. Whether as government agent or self-appointed agent of the godly cause, Carew's intervention literally inflamed the situation. After his arrival at Exeter, Carew discussed the crisis with the sheriff and JPs on 21 June. He then rode to Crediton with a small company to try to pacify the rebels. He found the town defended and they refused to negotiate. However, one of Carew's force set fire to the barns which formed part of the rebel defences. Wild panic ensued and the town was abandoned. This incident merely increased the distrust between gentry and commons: 'the noise of this fire and burning', related Hooker, 'was spread through the villages and the common people noised and spread it abroad that the gentlemen were altogether bent to overrun, spoil and destroy them'. Carew was later reprimanded in London for his provocative action.

The main army of the rebels moved round Exeter to Clyst St Mary, where, by 23 June, they had made camp and fortified the bridge on the Exeter road. The gentry then made another attempt to

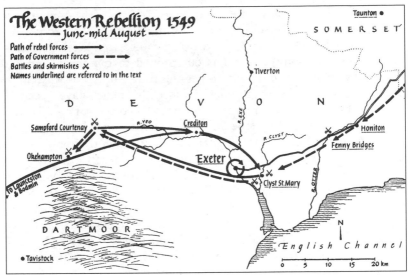

**The Western Rebellion 1549**
—— June-mid August ——
Path of rebel forces →
Path of Government forces ━ ━ ➤
Battles and skirmishes ✕
Names underlined are referred to in the text

Taunton •

SOMERSET

• Tiverton

D     E     V     O     N

Sampford Courtenay ✕     R.YEO     Crediton     R.EXE     Honiton ✕

Okehampton ✕     R.CLYST     Fenny Bridges

Exeter

Clyst St.Mary ✕

to Launceston Bodmin

DARTMOOR

• Tavistock

N

*English Channel*

0   5   10   15   20 km

*Map 2*

open negotiations. This time two of them, Sir Thomas Denys and Sir Hugh Pollard, were allowed into the village. They showed some sympathy with the rebels' demand that religion should remain as Henry VIII left it until Edward came of age. They extracted a promise from the commons that they would pursue their grievances by petition in an orderly manner. But Sir Peter Carew and Peter Courtenay, the sheriff, were dissatisfied with this, blaming Denys and Pollard 'for theire slender or rather synester dealinges'. That night, the commons, encouraged by this disagreement between the gentry, started to block the highways into Exeter. They were now determined to force Carew to hear their case. They took and imprisoned some of the Exeter merchants and gentry. Others left the city or 'secretelie kepte theireselffes close in certeyne howses then unknowne'. Carew himself escaped and took the road for London to impress on the government the gravity of the situation.

As late as 29 June Protector Somerset's response to the rising was still based on hopelessly inadequate information: his letter that day to Lord Russell, who had then just set out to attempt to restore order, was based on an impression that the rebellion was still confined to Sampford Courtenay. He knew nothing of the joint advance of Devonshire and Cornish contingents to Exeter. Somerset's resources were already strained. He was faced with enclosure riots in the midlands and south-east and feared that the French might take advantage of the opportunity offered by internal disorders to invade

[*Doc. 15*]. He was only able to provide Russell with a small and inadequate force. Russell found it difficult to enlist forces in Wiltshire and Somerset and dared not advance to Exeter. It seems that at this time a force that was determined to march on London would have had little difficulty in passing to the north of Russell by Bruton or to the south through Dorset. It might have received considerable additional strength as it approached the capital. Russell even talked of retreat: 'if we be driven to retire it standeth uncertayn to us hitherto by what quarter we shall most conveniently use the same until their determinations of proceeding more evidently appear'.

But the rebels were more concerned to demonstrate their seriousness by controlling the West Country than to appear in person before London. Perhaps the memory of Blackheath frightened them or perhaps the leaders' nerve failed at the prospect of advancing into unknown country. From Clyst, between 24 June and 2 July, they turned their faces back to Exeter. They sent a further and more detailed set of articles to the Council and coordinated their plans for a full-scale siege of the local capital [*Doc. 12*]. The leadership now consisted of three Cornish gentry, three Devon gentry and three commoners. On 2 July the rebels, 2,000 in number according to Hooker, advanced in procession on Exeter. They carried the banner of the Five Wounds, the pyx and censers. When the mayor refused their demand for support they surrounded the city. Somerset's letters show that at this time he was hopelessly out of touch with the situation. He continued to insist on appeasement. The siege of Exeter began while the government still hoped to remedy the situation by such stratagems as sending spies among the rebels to emphasize 'the terror of comytting treason, the feare of a kyng's execution'.

It was not until about 10 July that Somerset took the rebellion seriously enough to begin trying to divert some of his forces to help Russell. His answer to their articles, written on behalf of the king on 8 July, was a last attempt to persuade them of the error into which they had been led and to overawe them with the threat of vengeance. Meanwhile, Exeter was under siege and because the government's forces were so heavily committed elsewhere, six weeks went by before Russell could relieve it. The city was able to defy the rebels during that time because loyalty to the crown overcame religious conviction. There was a tradition of religious conservatism in Exeter. Hooker, who provides an eye-witness account of the siege, explains that the party 'of the old stamp and of the Romish religion' was larger than the Protestant group; on the other hand, the magistrates and chieftains of the city albeit they were not fully resolved and satisfied in religion yet they not respecting that but chiefly their dutifulness to the king and commonwealth, nothing liked the rebellion . . . but . . . do all things to defend the city and themselves against their rebellious attempts.

During the siege the citizens maintained contact with Russell through spies, but they were always in danger of being betrayed by one of their own number. A hundred citizens made a covenant to be about the city day and night to prevent any treachery. A plan by the Catholic party to allow the rebels in at a postern gate of the castle was only just discovered in time and two days before the city's deliverance the Catholics tried to raise a riot in the streets. Hooker emphasizes the tension between the two religious groups: when the mayor held a muster of all the commons in armour at the Guildhall rioting nearly broke out.

There were several violent clashes with the besiegers. When they tried to set fire to the gates the citizens used their ordnance against them charged with 'greate bagges of flynte stones and hayle shote'. A mine laid by the rebels under the city wall had to be flooded by a tinner. By the beginning of August there was danger of famine and the commons were 'verie impaciente to endure the countynual barkinge of theire hungrie bellies'. Morale was maintained by careful provision for poor relief which was organized by the mayor and aldermen.

Early in July Russell had advanced to Honiton but, short of money and men, he felt thoroughly insecure; 'having but a very small guard about him', says Hooker, 'he lived in more fear than was feared, for the rebels daily increased and his company decreased and shrank away and he not altogether assured of them which remained'. On 12 July Somerset had to report to Russell that the horsemen and footmen under Lord Grey that he had promised had been sent instead to deal with a 'sturr here in Bucks and Oxfordshire by instigacon of sundery preists for these matyers of religion'. Somerset was now alarmed; the rebellion in the west took second place to disturbances nearer the capital. But he no longer underestimated the extent of disloyalty in the west and appreciated Russell's anxiety and caution. He advised him not to trust the local gentry 'onles ye knowe them fully perswayded for the matier in contraversie of relygon'; he should 'wink at the matter' of Sir John Arundell who refused to bring forces to Russell's assistance from Dorset.

Russell, left to fend for himself, managed to get backing from three Exeter merchants to raise money through merchants of Taunton and Bristol. But his most serious problem remained the unwillingness of the men of Dorset and Somerset to join his army [*Doc. 16*]. He maintained in a letter to the Council on 18 July that, with only 1,000 footmen and 700 horses at the maximum, he could neither relieve the city nor resist a rebel advance. He constantly urged Somerset to send more forces. The Protector returned promises of assistance but again was forced to change his plans: the 'mayne force', at one time intended for the west under Lord Warwick, went instead to deal with Kett. By the end of July Somerset's attitude was hardening, or perhaps he was giving way to those on the Council who pressed him to abandon his policy of leniency [*Doc. 19*]. A harsher tone entered his letter to Russell on 27 July [*Doc. 16*].

Russell began his advance on 28 July. He forced an advance party of rebels to retire from Fenny Bridges after two engagements by the River Otter. The second, says Hooker, was 'sharp and cruel': Russell's men were caught at spoil by a new contingent of Cornishmen and 'many of them paied deerlie for their wares'. The rebels lost about 300 on this day. Russell continued his advance on 3 August when Lord Grey had arrived with his horsemen and 300 Italian mercenaries. This time the rebels defended Clyst St Mary with about 6,000 but again they were forced to abandon their position when the mercenaries fired the houses. The next day the final battle was fought on Clyst Heath, the besiegers of Exeter were drawn off and defeated, and those who escaped vanished quickly into the west-country lanes.

On 6 August Russell reached the walls of Exeter. The mayor came out to greet him and the king's standard of the red dragon was set up on the city walls. Hooker describes the city's joy; some died, he says, of overeating. Now at last Sir William Herbert arrived with 1,000 men, mainly Welshmen, and they helped gather in food and cattle for the city from the surrounding countryside. Russell followed Somerset's orders that he should make an example of the ringleaders, the more important of whom were to be sent to London, but pardon the common people involved in the rebellion. So Robert Welsh, the vicar of the church of St Thomas, was hanged on a gallows erected on his church tower in his vestments, with 'a holy-water bucket, a sprinkle, a sacring bell, a pair of beads and such other like popish trash hanged about him'.

Russell could proclaim the victory of Protestantism in Exeter but, despite his now formidable army, he did not feel sufficiently confident to advance into the disordered far west. The breakdown of local government in Devon and Cornwall had now lasted almost two months. Russell wrote to Somerset that to restore control it would be necessary to land 1,000 men at Plymouth 'at the backs of the rebells'. Then, while he delayed in Exeter during the second week of August, beset by problems of money and supplies, he heard that the rebels had re-established their camp at Sampford Courtenay. He was by this time being pressed by Somerset to dismiss at least some of his forces so that the gentry might be at home to defend the south-coast counties. With both the west and East Anglia in rebellion, the French declaration of war on 8 August had come at a moment of disturbing internal weakness. In a letter of 14 August Somerset warned that 'yf you shall suffer those rebells to breathe' they might make a further stand or even cooperate with a French invasion.

Somerset was unnecessarily worried since the rebels lacked the organization to hold Plymouth, which they had taken earlier in the summer, and were not even in contact with the French. But they showed courage and determination in facing the overwhelming royal army of about 8,000 men that marched west from Exeter on 16 August. The final struggle at Sampford Courtenay was prolonged. Arundell caught the royal troops in the rear and it required a threefold attack by Russell, Grey and Herbert in the evening to force the rebels to retire. Many were captured and killed in the chase that followed that night and in the engagements when groups of rebels turned to fight in Somerset and at Okehampton; about 4,000 west-country folk are said to have died at the hands of the royal army.

The rebellion never had a real chance of forcing the government to make concessions in its religious policy. Somerset might have been prepared to do so but under the stress of the sedition of the summer of 1549 he was rapidly losing his grip on the Council. Because the western rising coincided with the commotions in the east and south of England, its suppression was prolonged. At another time forces could have reached Exeter much more quickly and the rebellion might not have achieved the proportions or significance it did. Russell certainly faced a difficult task when he was sent to the west in June 1549, though there remain differences of view about how his performance there should be assessed [73 *pp. 453–77*; 133 *pp. 35–8*].

## THE CAUSES OF THE REBELLION

In her reassessment of the rebellion, Joyce Youings stated that 'the motives of most of those who took part are still very unclear' [140 *p. 100*]. In many ways this remains the most puzzling of all Tudor rebellions. We must consider the various sets of rebel demands in relation to the chronology of the rising. The first list of complaints, drawn up independently of the Cornishmen at Sampford Courtenay, can be reconstructed from the Protector's reply, which was printed on 8 July. The Devonshire rebels disliked being expected to receive 'common bread' rather than wafers at the mass and they objected to the new form which services took in the Prayer Book. They expected the Latin tongue to be retained. They did not want their children to have to wait until they reached years of discretion to be confirmed. They wanted the Act of Six Articles reimposed and all Henry VIII's statutes to be enforced until Edward VI came of age. This first manifesto, in other words, was a lay protest against changes in religious practices and rituals that touched deep emotions in a small inland market town.

Yet already, at this stage of the rebellion, there is good reason to think that more than just religion was involved. In his letter of 26 June Somerset responded to a request from the Devon magistrates for a delay in the execution of a new statute imposing new taxes on goods, including a poll tax on sheep and a tax on the sale of woollen cloth [*Doc. 15*]. These taxes had both a fiscal and a social purpose: Somerset needed money for his intended war against the Scots and he wanted to discourage the enclosure which went with large-scale sheep farming. Devon, long an enclosed county, was likely to be hit particularly hard because the rate of the tax on sheep kept on enclosed pasture had been set higher than on those kept on commons. Most Devon farmers kept some sheep. The census of sheep had been scheduled to start on 1 May 1549 and there is evidence that, in some parishes near Exeter at least, the numbering had begun before the rising broke out. 'He had heard of rumours circulating in Devon', Somerset told Russell on 29 June, that 'after the payment for shepe they should paie for theyre geese and pigs and such like'. Rumour-mongering of the kind that affected Lincolnshire in 1536 also seems to have played its part in Devon in 1549.

The second set of articles was drawn up by the combined Devon and Cornish host, probably very soon after the beginning of the siege of Exeter on 2 July [140 *pp. 108–9*]. Its content can be reconstructed from a draft answer written in London. The programme by this stage had become broader and there was a particular emphasis on some of the inadequacies of the parish clergy. They were accused of failing to explain the new liturgy to their flocks and it was implied that their concern to gather fees had led to some withholding baptism and burial services. The Cornish demanded a liturgy in their own language (which was still widely spoken) and it was suggested that the Treason Act of 1534 should be restored. The tax on sheep and cloth was now explicitly mentioned and measures were requested to counter dearth of victuals.

The final version of the rebels' manifesto was prepared later in July. In this case we do have a reliable copy [*Doc. 12*]. These articles were sent up to London on 27 July by the correspondent Mr R.L., a gentleman who was at that time at Lord Russell's camp near Ottery St Mary. R.L.'s letter, part of which is reproduced [*Doc. 13*], is a vital source because it gives us some impression of the disputes and confusions which were evidently rife in the rebel camp: 'such diversities of heades there were amonges them that for every kynde of brayn there was one maner of article'. He was clear that the common people were grieved by the impact of inflation, that the priests had their own very specific interests to pursue and that the rebellion had attracted a considerable riff-raff, those he called the 'seedmen of sedicion'. But it is the impact of the conservative clergy that shows through most clearly in the manifesto itself. Their dislike of the new theology is evident in the demand that all books of scripture in English should be called in, their sacerdotalism in the insistence on exclusion of laymen from communicating except at Easter and then only in one kind. Whereas there was a new reference to the restoration of abbey lands, three earlier items – the Treasons Act, the sheep tax and food prices – were now omitted. The demand that has caused most debate is number 13, the call for a limitation on the number of servants to be employed by gentlemen. This may have been an expression of resentment at the influence which some gentry, perhaps particularly those who were Protestants, exercised over those they employed. 'They understand that servynge men be comenly brought up in such civilite that hardely they be made traytours', wrote R.L., 'yt is a comon proverbe that trust servynge man trust gentyll man.'

Later the German exile reformer Martin Bucer told a correspondent abroad that the rebels had gathered up all the copies of the Prayer Book which they could find and burnt them in their camp [88 *p. 430*]. It was therefore not surprising that the Council regarded the rebellion as primarily religious in purpose, and that this was the preoccupation of various replies to the rebel demands. The most lengthy was written by an evangelical Devon layman, Philip Nichols: in his most emotive passage Nichols rehearsed the familiar argument that rebellion leads to anarchy. Archbishop Cranmer's tirade was full of his anger at the rebels' presumption in addressing their sovereign so brazenly, as well as their superstitious ignorance about religion [88 *pp. 440–1*].

The voice of the convinced Protestant who sincerely believed in the new order sounds most clearly in Nichols's impressive tract. In answer to the ambiguous reference to 'our forefathers' in the first article he put forward the authority of Moses and the prophets; to the councils of the medieval church he opposed the Councils of the Apostles [*Doc. 12*]. He then derided the rebels' rash pronouncements against heresy, which he said they did not understand. Cranmer maintained that the first article was traitorous and contradicted in its support for Rome 'the old ancient laws and customs of this realm'. It was inspired, he said, by the priests' desire for benefit of clergy: 'If a priest had slain one of your sons or brethren, that you should have no remedy against him, but only before the bishop.' Nichols took up the theme of the self-interest of the priesthood in his comments on the Six Articles which the rebels would have had restored (article 2). He attacked the 'mischief wrought' by 'their confession auricular' and 'their sacrament of the altare' and descended quickly to crude anticlerical propaganda: with the end of auricular confession 'is cut from them all opportunity of moving men's wives to folly, of enticing men's daughters to lewdness and vice'. Nichols then contrasted the chasteness of clerical marriage, advocated in the scriptures as 'holy and honourable afore God', with the fornication practised by priests. He argued that the Six Articles constituted a temporary measure now abrogated by consent of the whole realm through parliament.

It was not difficult for Nichols and Cranmer to ridicule the conservatism expressed by articles 3 and 8. 'Had you rather', asked Cranmer, 'be like pies or parrots, that be taught to speak, and yet understand not one word what they say, than be true christian men that pray unto God in heart and faith?' Surely, they both scornfully asked, there were more Cornishmen who understood English than Latin. If they had made a humble petition to the king to have the new service translated into Cornish, Nichols told the rebels, they might have achieved their purpose. 'But', he went on, harking back to their presumption, 'we Cornishmen utterly refuse this new English were too much for a parishioner to say to his curate, or a neighbour to his constable; much more too much it is for subjects so to say to any rulers or governors.' Cranmer tried to show the rebels that the Catholic rituals they were used to were much more like the games and pastimes of the Christmas season than the new service which was based on scripture: 'the priest speaking aloud in Latin, and some walking up and down in the church, some saying other prayers in Latin, and none understandeth other'.

The government writers set about condemning the ritualism (article 4) and superstition (article 7) of the rebels by citing biblical passages and decrees of the early Church. Pope Honorius III, Cranmer agreed, had decreed that the sacrament should be reserved in order that the priest could take it to the sick, but he had not mentioned hanging it over the altar. This, Nichols maintained, was merely a convenient solution to the problem of keeping the sacrament when 'by negligence of the curates and parsons, some times it moulded and putrified, sometimes it was eaten up with myce or other vermin'. It was never 'decreed by any constitution of the Church'. Yet the western rebels would have had all who would not consent to this practice to 'dye lyke heretykes'. To refute the demand for annual communion by the laity (article 5) Nichols quoted extensively from the decrees of general Councils to show that 'Christian men ought to go very often to the most holy communion'. Cranmer attacked holy water (article 7) as a superstition fabricated by the Papacy. He quoted the second commandment to show that image worship was idolatry. The ninth article, on masses for the dead, touches on a crucial doctrinal issue. It is interesting that it relates to a belief that impinged closely on the lives of both laity and clergy. For laypeople, the naming of lost friends and relations in church offered comfort and hope; for clergy the dissolutions of 1548 had deprived them of a valuable vested interest. Nichols answered this article by expounding predestination doctrine: 'As for change of God's sentence and judgment there can none be after this life. But (as the scripture saith) where every tree falleth there shall it bee.'

The rebels' objection to the open Bible (article 10), clearly inspired by the priests, provided Nichols with another opportunity to display his militant Protestantism. He vigorously attacked the Catholic priests who had led the people to 'embrace superstition and idolatory for true worship of God, the puddleway and suddes of mennes tradicions for the pure and clere fountain of the Apostles' ordinances'. The rebels' insistence that Dr Moreman should be sent to minister to them (article 11) was probably due to the energy he had shown when, as Vicar of Menheniot in Henry VIII's reign, he had kept a school there. He had been active in teaching the people the Lord's Prayer, the Ten Commandments and the Creed in accordance with Cromwell's injunctions. But Cranmer severely reminded the rebels that it was not the office of a godly prince to give the people teachers who, through their Catholicism, would corrupt them. In the 1530s it had been possible for Cromwell to activate both conservatives and radicals in improving the people's religious knowledge. But by 1549, as the attitudes on both sides of this conflict illustrate, the lines of division had hardened.

Analysis of the rebel articles then suggests that this rising was principally religious but that economic discontents were also involved. A closer look at the leadership of the rising in the context of the social and religious structure of western society will enable us to extend this argument. It is worth noting first that Professor Youings claims very plausibly that she may have discovered 'the real leader of the rebels for whom we have hitherto sought in vain, the compiler of the fifteen articles and the one man capable of holding the disparate company together' [140 *p. 121*]. This was Robert Welsh, the vicar of the parish of St Thomas just outside Exeter. He was a strong man, a good wrestler and a good shot with the longbow and the crossbow. More importantly, he was a Cornish-man, a native of Penryn; thus he was the ideal man to bridge the traditionally wide gap between the people of Cornwall and of Devon, and unite them in a common cause. He was clearly a man whom the rebels looked to, most of them far from home, during the long and arduous siege of Exeter. Lord Russell singled him out for trial by martial law and execution. He was charged, John Hooker tells us, with persuading 'the people to the contemnynge of the reformed religion accordinge to the kinges proceadinges' and with being a 'captayne and pryncypall dealer in the cause of the rebellion'.

Clearly there were others besides Welsh who directed the siege of Exeter. It is impossible to account for the length of the siege and the effectiveness with which Russell's soldiers were beaten off unless one supposes a degree of yeoman and minor gentry leadership. Some of the leading men of this kind of status, like Humphrey Arundell and John Winslade, have already been mentioned. Among the others were Thomas or William Underhill (accounts of his first name differ) and William Segar who both came from families of some substance in Sampford Courtenay. Little more can be discovered about such men but there are tantalizing hints that the leadership of the rebellion bore some relation to the Courtenay affinity, the clan whose conservative manoeuvrings in the south-west had come to nothing in the 1530s. Robert Smyth of St Germans, for example, who was allegedly involved shortly before 1549 in an assault on the house of the Protestant vicar of St Stephens-by-Saltash, was married to a Courtenay.

Some of the rebel articles may be adduced in favour of the argument that, though it is now hard to document, there may have been a polarization in the west in 1549 between a clique of quite radically Protestant gentry on the one hand and the remains of the Courtenay clan on the other. Philip Nichols enjoyed the patronage of Sir Peter Carew and was the antagonist in print of the Exeter canon Richard Crispin, whose release from the Tower was sought in the rebel articles. Why did the rebels call for the pardon and recall of Cardinal Reginald Pole? He had been closely associated with Henry Courtenay, the Marquess of Exeter, who was executed in 1538. Crispin had been a chaplain to the Marquess and had been involved in 1534 in the affair of the Nun of Kent. John Bury, one of those who signed the articles, had been in the Marquess's service. According to R.L., he 'setteth forth the matter of the Cardinal so much, as indeed he maketh no other matter'. Two gentry from the magisterial class, who did their utmost to treat with the rebels and certainly regarded them very differently from Carew, also had Courtenay connections. Sir Thomas Denys was accused by Thomas Cromwell in 1537 of hanging at the Courtenay sleeve. Anthony Harvey was a former surveyor of the Marquess and some time after the rebellion was to be the Marchioness's sole executor.

The division of west-country society in 1549 undoubtedly ran deep. It seems very likely that family alliances and political memories played a part in sustaining this curiously perplexing rebellion. But there seems little doubt also that it drew its popular strength from people's fears that the government was deliberately destroying traditional spiritual ways and from rumours about new taxes which had either been enacted or were simply imagined.

# 6 KETT'S REBELLION AND SOUTHERN ENGLAND

## THE COMMOTIONS: MAY–AUGUST 1549

In May, trouble about the enclosure of common land started breaking out in Wiltshire, Somerset and Bristol; the protests were enlarged by crassly violent retaliation, particularly by Sir William Herbert of Wilton. A mark of how widespread and sudden they then became is that different contemporary commentators confidently said that they first began variously in Hertfordshire, Northamptonshire, Suffolk or Kent, and there are further records of them in Hampshire, Surrey and elsewhere [88 *pp. 429–31*]. Protector Somerset then frantically tried to undo the harm done through the initial harshness by ostentatiously seeking conciliation with the protesters; a royal proclamation at the end of May, promising redress of grievances, may have been one factor in producing a temporary calm. The government's attention was then abruptly diverted to the far more threatening outbreak in the West Country.

Throughout a dangerously sunny June, southern England outside the new Devon–Cornwall rebellion remained in what the Earl of Arundel in Surrey described as 'a quavering quiet', but this peace suddenly and dramatically collapsed at the beginning of July. On 1 July the government summoned a long list of nobility and gentry from the Thames Valley and the home counties to meet at, or send representatives to, Windsor Castle, probably in order to create an army to go westward. It may have been popular observation of these agitated preparations among the better sort that precipitated what happened next.

On 20 June 1549 a crowd from three villages around Attleborough in Norfolk had thrown down the hedges of a local landlord who had enclosed part of their common land. This proved not to be the last echo of the May stirs, but the foretaste of something new. The former abbey church in the nearby market town of Wymondham was dedicated to Our Lady and Thomas Becket, and the whole neighbourhood gathered at Wymondham for a play to commemorate the feast of the translation of Becket's relics between 6 and 8 July. Crowds threw down hedges in nearby villages, including those of John Flowerdew, one of many successful lawyers among Norfolk gentry. Flowerdew was unpopular in Wymondham because at the dissolution of the abbey he had begun demolishing the eastern parts of the abbey church, those not used by the townsfolk. The inhabitants wanted to preserve the whole church for the town's services, and had in fact bought the eastern parts from the crown.

The manor of Wymondham was held of the Earl of Warwick by Robert Kett, whose family had settled there in 1483. He was a tanner by trade but he and his brother William, a butcher, were also substantial landowners. Flowerdew hoped to exploit the commons' mood of aggressiveness by persuading them to throw down the hedges of an enclosure of common land Kett had made nearby. His intention was to pursue his feud with the Ketts, who were closely associated with the church he had looted. But the commons found in Robert Kett a leader rather than another victim. Kett agreed that the common land he had enclosed should be thrown open again and, though his own interest in the enclosure conflict clearly lay with the landlords, said he would stand by the rioters until they had obtained their rights. He now showed himself an inspired leader. He decided to march to Norwich and rapidly gained support on the way. He arrived outside the city on 10 July to find that the news of his coming had led some of the poorer citizens to destroy the hedge round the town close, where the freemen grazed their cattle. By 12 July he had set up camp on Mousehold Heath, a large open hillside just outside the city walls. Within a few days the camp was said to number 16,000.

Traditionally, this Norfolk story has been told in isolation, because of its dramatic and uniquely tragic outcome, and because we have a flood of detailed, if partisanly hostile, narrative about it. This, however, hides the fact that with astonishing speed from 7 July and during the following week, mass uprisings swept through precisely the areas from which gentry had been summoned to Windsor on 1 July – the Thames Valley, the home counties, and also north to the furthest reaches of East Anglia. In Norfolk, another camp in the north-west at Castle Rising moved to Downham Market, where a camp was in existence by 15 July; a further camp was set up in central Norfolk at Hingham. In Suffolk, by 14 July a camp had been set up outside Ipswich and was

# Kett's Rebellion
## ——1549——

0   5   10   15   20km

- - - - - County boundary
- - - - - - Boundary of sheep-corn and
wood-pasture farming areas
Places with camps are underlined

N

• Binham

• Little Walshingham

•Castle Rising   N O R F O L K

•King's
Lynn   •Gayton Thorpe   •North Elmham
HUNDRED OF
LAUNDITCH

Norwich   Great
Yarmouth

HUNDRED OF   Bowthorpe•
• Downham   SOUTH GREENHOE   •Hethersett
Market   Morley   •Wymondham

•Attleborough   HUNDRED OF   Lowestoft
EARSHAM
Wilby•
Kenninghall   Earsham•   •Bungay   Carlton
Brandon   HUNDRED OF GUILTCROSS   Colville
•Bressingham

S U F F O L K
Cavenham•   Peasenhall•
Gazeley   Bury St. Edmunds   •Westleton
•Westley   Kenton•   Framlingham   •Kelsale
Earl Soham•   •Leiston
•Crowfield   Benhall•
Stowmarket•   Aldeburgh•
•Otley
Lavenham
Haverhill   •Brent   Melton   •Orford
Eleigh   Akenham•   Ipswich
•Sudbury   •Brightwell
•Nacton
•Bures   •Walton
•Landguard

*Map 3*

dispensing justice to the people. Another camp at Bury St Edmunds probably came into existence about the same time. It was only at Cambridge and Great Yarmouth that the authorities were at once able to halt the rising. In Kent 'the rebellion of Commonwealth' set up camps at Canterbury and outside Maidstone, under a leader called Latimer (no connection with Bishop Hugh Latimer), who styled himself 'the Commonwealth of Kent' [1]. These camps were so characteristic of the commotions that already, on 19 July in the

Thames Valley, Sir Thomas Smith described those involved as 'the camp men' [84 *p. 47*].

The gentry were caught unawares: many were away in London or had obeyed the royal summons to Windsor. Those who were at home were powerless in the face of massive demonstrations that show unmistakable signs of coordination and planning. The sites chosen for the camps were predictable ones often associated with government. Bury was the capital of west Suffolk, as Norwich was of eastern and central Norfolk and Canterbury of Kent. The insurgents in east Suffolk moved their original camp outside Ipswich, at some stage in July, to the village of Melton near Woodbridge, a long-established administrative centre of the dean and chapter of Ely's liberty of St Audrey. More than a thousand people seem to have camped at Melton: one foraging expedition brought back 320 sheep and 4,000 rabbits [84 *p. 44*]. Led by tradesmen and yeomen, the countrymen of Norfolk and Suffolk set up a remarkable quadrilateral of camps in July 1549, challenging the traditional rulers of these shires. For many years after there was talk of 'the camping time' of 1549: indeed, as late as 1596, Kentish people were talking of setting up a camp to remedy local grievances [132 *p. 92*]. Kett's Norwich camp was the best organized, but the full dimensions of the movement need to be understood if we are to see its real significance.

In Norwich Nicholas Sotherton's narrative tells of disagreement as to what attitude should be adopted towards a camp of demonstrators who were perhaps greater in numbers than the population within the walls. Those who, like Thomas Codd the mayor, urged moderation, argued that it was unlawful to collect a force without the king's command even to put down rebellion. Anyhow it was impractical; within the city a substantial number of people were sympathetic to Kett. So Codd, the popular evangelical preacher Robert Watson and Thomas Aldrich, a man much respected and, says Sotherton, 'of good wisdom and honesty', did their best to cooperate with Kett in his demands for provisions for his camp from the city. Sotherton naturally emphasizes the restraining influence they were able to have on the hotheads of the camp who looked for further chances to riot. The organization of the camp and its commissariat depended on the authority of Kett. Codd, Aldrich and Watson, though, also signed his commission to men to bring in all manner of cattle and provision of victual, and Codd and Aldrich signed the demands which Kett drew up to present to Protector Somerset [*Doc. 17*]. On 21 July York Herald arrived from the government to offer pardon to the rebels if they dispersed. Now the city authorities felt strong enough to act on their own. The mayor and gentry prepared to defend the city. Aldermen and their servants kept watch at the gates and six pieces of ordnance were hauled into position on the walls.

The insurgents meanwhile had brought in cannon from coastal defences. On the night the Herald arrived they began their bombardment. This was ineffective because they could do little harm from the top of the hill and when they brought the cannon down nearer the city walls the next morning they feared to use it as they were within range of the city shot. The next day (22 July), the camp men called for a truce. But when the aldermen refused this, they made a full assault armed with spears, swords and pitchforks. Sotherton's attempt to excuse the failure of city archers to repel the attack is unconvincing and illustrates his characteristic desire to vilify the rebel camp:

> So impudent were they and so desperate that of theyr vagabond boyes (wyth reverens spoken) brychles and bear arssyde came emong the thickett of the arrows and gathered them up when some of the arrows stuck fast in theyr leggs and other parts and did therewith most shamefully turne up their bare tayles agenst those which did shoote, whych soe dysmayed the archers that it tooke theyr hart from them.

By that evening Norwich was in the insurgents' hands and the Herald had left for London, after a second failure in proclaiming pardon to the contemptuous crowd. Kett ordered the arrest of Codd, Aldrich and Watson who were now kept prisoner at Surrey Place, the late Earl of Surrey's mansion on Mousehold Heath of which they had taken possession. But in view of their influence in the city, they were allowed some liberty and were treated decently.

The government had much less difficulty in quelling the Suffolk rising. Sir Anthony Wingfield, a local magnate who was also a Privy Councillor, managed to persuade those encamped at Melton that the king would pardon them. They went home full of hopes of better times. Most of those taken prisoner were soon discharged and the only execution in Suffolk was in connection with the bridgehead that the people at Downham had established at Brandon on the Norfolk border. Yet twenty years later a Lavenham man spoke bitterly of the events of 1549: 'we wyll not be deceyved as we were at the laste rysinge, for then we were promised ynoughe and more then ynoughe. But the more was an hawlter' [84 *pp. 45–7*].

Neutralizing Kett and his camp was not so simple. An expeditionary force under the Marquis of Northampton reached Norwich on 30 July: his mishandling of the situation was unique in the various confrontations with the south-eastern rebels that summer. The presence in his company of several of the leading Suffolk gentry suggests that he had succeeded in neutralizing the Bury St Edmunds camp on his way: they would hardly have left their own neighbourhood if western Suffolk was still in commotion. Northampton wasted time: he did not take any immediate initiative towards Mousehold but allowed himself to be feasted and entertained by Augustine Steward, the deputy acting for Mayor Codd during the emergency. The Italian mercenaries Northampton had brought with him 'rested in their armore uppon cushions and pillows'. Meanwhile the camp men managed to capture one of these Italians, 'gorgeously apparelled' who was hanged over the walls of Surrey Place, stripped naked to show contempt for his foreign finery, and fury at the employment of mercenaries against Englishmen.

After frantic strengthening of the city defences during the night, Northampton's trumpeter declared a pardon from the walls to any who would give themselves up. Only about twenty came down the hill. The Mousehold army then made a determined attack into the city and a bloody battle followed around the precincts of the cathedral close. St Martin-at-Palace parish register records the burial of thirty-six men who died; among them was Lord Sheffield, killed by a butcher named Fulke. Northampton left the city in disarray. He had succeeded in turning a vast popular demonstration into a full-scale rebellion, when everywhere else the commotions had been defused.

Panic followed among the gentry: 'Some fled in theyr doublets and hosen and some in there lightest garments beste to escape and make haste away', relates Sotherton. Once more the rebels were in control of the city and during the next three weeks Kett maintained his camp at Mousehold with the enforced cooperation of the Norwich city leaders. He was sufficiently confident to try to extend his support by winning over Yarmouth. First he sent a small force to persuade them to join him. When they refused, he attacked the town, but he achieved little apart from the destruction of some harbour work in progress; thirty rebels were taken prisoner and six of their guns were lost. It was Kett's first setback.

Meanwhile the government had issued commissions to all shires around Norfolk for levying troops; the Earl of Warwick was put in command of the new force, said to be of 12,000 men, again including many mercenaries, which arrived outside Norwich on 23 August. A band of rebels met Warwick's herald and rode with him through the city to Mousehold where the camp was ready in good order to hear his speech. 'They put of theyr caps and cryed God Save King Edward', says Sotherton. The herald offered pardon to all except Robert Kett himself. Despite this the rebel leader was prepared to go with the herald to meet the Earl of Warwick. But some of his followers pulled their leader back saying, according to Holinshed, that the man 'was not the king's herald but someone made out by the gentlemen in such a gaie coate, patched together of vestments and church stuffe, being sent only to deceive them, in offering them pardon'. Distrust of the herald turned to anger and tumult when the cry went up that a boy had been killed by one of the soldiers. The moment when peace had seemed possible had passed.

The next day Warwick and his army entered Norwich and hanged some of the rebels whom they found in the city. The rebels, in a daring coup on the night of 23 August, captured some of Warwick's ordnance, attacking the carts with staves and pitchforks, and they were able to use these guns for the next three days. Otherwise, their tactics against the army in Norwich were arson at night and back-street skirmishing in the daytime, and at first Warwick's army seemed as vulnerable and confused as Parr's had been. However, on 26 August more than a thousand more foreign mercenaries arrived and Warwick had by then cut some of the camp's supply lines. Kett perhaps then realized that the tide was turning against him. According to Sotherton, he became desperate and 'trusted uppon faynid prophecies which were phantastically devised':

The countrie gruffes, Hob, Dick and Hick
with clubs and clowted shoone,
Shall fill up Dussindale with blood
of slaughtered bodies soon.

This was the prophecy, Holinshed reports, which Kett followed on the evening of 26 August, although it foretold the disaster which was to overwhelm the rebels at Dussindale the next day. The well-fortified positions at Mousehold were abandoned and fired and the ordnance was moved to Dussindale, where trenches were dug and a defensive position prepared. Warwick was thus presented with a magnificent chance to use his cavalry. Sir Edmund Knyvet was sent to ask the rebels to yield, but their defiance was emphasized by shots which wounded the royal standard-bearer and killed his horse from under him. However, this was their last success. Professional soldiers quickly broke their front line, and Sotherton reports that Kett panicked and fled, only to be quickly arrested next morning. When the news of his capture spread, the continuing desperate rebel resistance crumbled. Perhaps as many as 3,000 of Kett's forces were killed.

Kett was condemned for treason on 26 November and hanged at Norwich Castle on 7 December. His brother William was hanged from Wymondham steeple. Although Neville states that 300 in all were executed, there is only clear evidence of forty-nine paying the penalty for rebellion. For Kett, the turning-point had been the arrival of the herald on 21 July, with his summons to the camp to disperse. Up till then he believed in the government's sympathy. In the disillusion that followed he could not prevent the unprovoked attack on the city. The extinction of the rebellion became only a matter of time [*73 pp. 477–93*].

The disorders of Edward VI's reign did not end at Dussindale. Popular unrest continued: the Privy Council register reveals commotions in 1550 in the west, Nottinghamshire, Kent and elsewhere, which were serious enough for the men of the dissolved Boulogne garrison to be distributed in the disaffected counties. In spring 1551 there was more widespread trouble, and in August 1551 insurrection began in Leicestershire, Northamptonshire and Rutland, by certain 'light knaves, horsecoursers and craftsmen', as was reported to Lord Admiral Clinton [*74 pp. 56–69, 427–34*]. In the short term, the summer commotions led to a very different sort of upheaval: the overthrow of Protector Somerset by his colleagues on the Privy Council. His efforts to bring the commotions to an end by conciliating the rebels of eastern England had been bitterly resented by many local rulers, and events seemed to prove that his habitual arrogance was not balanced by success in government. The Earl of Warwick's return from Norfolk provided a convincing leader for opposition from a curious combination of evangelicals and religious conservatives, united only by their conviction that Somerset must go.

Matters were brought to a head at the end of August by French raids which captured various forts around Boulogne, a symbol of national pride and of old King Henry's victory over the hereditary national enemy. There were even strong rumours that after this defeat, Somerset was willing to hand back the whole of Henry's great prize to France. Late in September Somerset made the bad mistake of quarrelling with Warwick. He brusquely refused extra rewards above their wages to the English and foreign troops who had been operating in East Anglia; he had already annoyed Warwick by the tight financial rein which he had kept over the expedition. This was coupled with a proclamation in the name of King, Protector and Council on 30 September peremptorily ordering all the soldiers out of London to various assigned posts, now that their wages had been paid. Within a day or two, Warwick had summoned dissident Councillors to meet without Somerset, and he had also ensured that if necessary he would have the backing of the foreign mercenaries whom he had brought from East Anglia. Sensing the build-up of forces against him, Somerset panicked; in the end it was he rather than the dissident Councillors who escalated the situation and on 5 October openly tried to use force to maintain his position. After that, it took just over a week to persuade him that he had gone too far and that he had no substantial backing: the end of his Protectorship followed, to general relief that yet more blood had not been spilled [88 *pp. 443–6*].

## THE CAUSES OF THE COMMOTIONS

In a proclamation of 14 June 1549, Edward VI's government pardoned the 'great number of rude and ignorant people' who had 'riotously assembled themselves, plucked down men's hedges' and 'disparked their parks'. These disorders arose from the unrealistic social policy of Somerset, which was by this time coming under severe criticism [*Doc. 19*]. His genuine concern to protect the commons from exploitation is proved by the private Act of Parliament he promoted to give security to copyholders on his own estates. He also established a court of requests in his own house to give justice to the poor. But his patronage of the reformist-minded government administrator John Hales, who introduced three bills on enclosure into parliament in 1548, quickly aroused the fierce opposition of the landlords and Somerset was forced to resort to administrative action. By 1549 rumours of proceedings in the midlands by Hales's enclosure commission were spreading to neighbouring counties. The idea that the government supported the commons in redressing their own grievances, that the 'Good Duke' was on their side, encouraged them to riot. But why was the Attleborough riot followed by one of the major rebellions of the Tudor period? Obviously, enclosure was only one element in Kett's rebellion. Three main aspects of the rising demand analysis: protest against bad government, agrarian grievances in the region and articles of Kett's manifesto that relate to the clergy and religion [84].

The rebellion was led by men just outside the orbit of the governing classes in town and countryside. Both the behaviour of those who camped and the articles issued by Kett show that one of their prime objects was to express their dissatisfaction at the way East Anglia was being governed. Kett believed the government in London was on his side. His purpose (article 27) was to ensure that the 'good lawes, statutes, proclamacions' made for the people were no longer disregarded by the JPs. The Mousehold Heath camp sought to demonstrate, and did so remarkably effectively for a few weeks, that the county could be fairly governed. Local officers responded. The churchwardens of Carlton Colville collected monies and carried them off to the new administrative centre at Mousehold; the parish officers at North Elmham kept a careful record of their payments about business under Kett's direction. When the rebels combed the Norfolk villages for food they carried commissions signed by Kett and sent out in the king's name. 'John of Great Yarmouth' was ordered 'to repair home and bring with you, with as much speed as may be, a last of beer, to maintain your pour neighbours withal, and if any man disturb or let you in this business, he shall suffer imprisonment of body'.

The activities of the Suffolk camps confirm the impression that the rebellion was an attack on self-interested and irresponsible men in local government and that its leaders exhibited a concern for justice. The captain of the Bury camp put George Swinbourne, whose stepchildren's property was claimed by another, into possession. What is clear is the sense of alienation felt by the leaders of the rising from their immediate social superiors; moreover, Kett's manifesto leaves a strong impression of the desire to recapture a past world where everyone knew his place and function. The leading gentry were recognized as having certain privileges, such as those of keeping their own dovecots and rabbit warrens (articles 10 and 23). In return they were expected to preserve traditional social boundaries: lords of manors should not be bailiffs to other lords (article 25), gentry should not be holders of spiritual livings (article 26). Two articles were aimed at lawyers, men like John Flowerdew of Hethersett and John Corbet of Sprowston, who had his home and dovecot pillaged by the rebels. The offices of feodary and escheator gave men exceptional opportunities for benefiting interested parties. The escheator for the past year had been Flowerdew, whose feud with Kett has already been mentioned. Article 12 is actually a demand that royal rights should be protected against corrupt local officials: the feodary, the county representative of the Court of

Wards, who was responsible for all matters relating to land held of the king by knight service, must not enter collusive agreements with tenants-in-chief when he 'found the office', in other words, declared what estate the tenant held. If he was popularly elected (a striking demand in the case of a royal official), an honest man would be chosen. The intention behind article 18 was to save poorer tenants from the expenses involved in an inquisition into their property such as the escheator or feodary might demand.

The events at Norwich in July and August 1549 indicate a breakdown of trust between the governing class and the people who normally sustained local government that has no parallel in the Tudor period: distrust between the western rebels and a Protestant section of the gentry was an element in the protracted dislocation of Devon in the same year, but there social and governmental relationships never became the central issue that they were in East Anglia [84]. Social tension was undoubtedly very strong in Norwich at the time of the rebellion. The city's marked inequality of wealth made it vulnerable to class antagonisms when times seemed bad. About 6 per cent of the population owned approximately 60 per cent of the land and goods. The subsidy assessment of 1525 shows that this group included the men whose viewpoint Sotherton represented, like Thomas Aldrich and Augustine Steward. While Thomas Aldrich was assessed as worth £700 and was the second wealthiest man in the city, about 35 per cent of the citizens were too poor to pay even the minimum of four pence. By the 1540s the worsted industry was in decline and some craftsmen were emigrating: in May 1549 the Common Council complained that 'foreigners' and beggars were replacing those who were leaving. The instability of Norwich society at a time of economic readjustment helps to explain the ease with which Kett took control of the city.

East Anglia's social tension by and large found its expression through the humiliation of local gentry rather than through direct violence. Four men whose fathers had been or currently were JPs in Suffolk were rounded up and kept as prisoners at the Melton camp. The story of Richard Wharton's uncomfortable return to the city of Norwich [*Doc. 18*] may be somewhat dramatized in Sotherton's account but it captures the atmosphere of the rebel camp. There was also the deliberate use of public nakedness as a means of derision. Sotherton's account of the rebels' 'bear arssyde' behaviour has already been quoted (p. 68). There were also specific outbreaks of uncontrolled popular anger, like the killing of the Italian mercenary captain; the door of the city's treasure house, someone noted later in the Chamberlain's accounts, was 'sore hewyn and mankyld by traitor Ket and his Kytlings'. Yet most of the time Kett retained a good deal of discipline.

An understanding of the overall agricultural structure of Norfolk and Suffolk is essential to establishing the ambiguous role of enclosure in the rising. There were two regions of light soils where a combination of pastoral and arable farming was practised: dung from large sheep flocks provided the necessary fertility to the soil for high grain yields. One sheep-corn area lay along the east Suffolk coast from Landguard Point to Yarmouth; the other stretched from north-west Suffolk into northern Norfolk (see Map 3, p. 66). Between these two areas of light soils was one of heavier soils: this ran across central Suffolk into south-eastern Norfolk. This area was quite heavily wooded and was largely devoted to pasture farming. It was here that enclosure was a prominent grievance – specifically the enclosure of common land. For instance, the inhabitants of Hingham (where a camp was established) had taken their landlord Sir Henry Parker to Star Chamber for infringement of their rights of common pasture on an area of wasteland in the village. Failing to receive satisfaction, they threatened him with violence and said they would kill the 600 sheep with which he had overstocked the commons. Parker brought an indictment for riot against the tenants at the quarter sessions, where they maintained they had common rights as well for 'sheep as for greate beasts'. The defence of common land emerges clearly as a crucial issue in Kett's manifesto (articles 3 and 11). It can be related particularly to the resentment felt against landlords in the wood pasture region where the recorded incidents of throwing open enclosures all took place.

In the sheep-corn districts, people's attitude to enclosure was quite different. There the East Anglian custom of the foldcourse made it possible for gentry to establish and sustain large sheep flocks by using their tenants' holdings. The custom had developed from the medieval right of foldage, by which landlords could demand that tenants should manure their demesne land by folding flocks of sheep on it at night. Through the foldcourse, the obverse of this, they had a right to pasture their own flocks on their tenants' lands and on common land. This system was likely to reverse the attitude of the manorial lord and his tenant towards enclosing. There were obvious advantages for the tenant in enclosing his land as a means of excluding the landlord's sheep from using his pasture. Thus we find Robert Browne of Leiston in Suffolk involved in litigation with the tenants at the time of the 1549 rebellion over the enclosures they had made. The rebels at the Melton camp made Browne one of their main targets. Some 320 of his sheep were carried off, his servants were imprisoned and his wife and family had to hide in the woods; Browne only escaped molestation himself because he was away from home at the time [84 *pp. 50–3*].

It is no surprise to find that the rebel articles included a demand that the wealthier gentry should not be allowed to 'graze nor fede eny bullocks or shepe . . . but only for the provicion of his house'. Thomas Townshend was typical of the men earning substantial fortunes at the expense of peasant rights. He built up a flock of 4,000 sheep in the 1540s and his accounts show that his total profits steadily increased from £99 in 1545 to £133 in 1548 [56; 116]. The Townshends used the foldcourse system as a first step towards purchase of their tenants' rights, often in dubiously legal ways, or eviction. In this way they expanded their own permanent pasture [98 *pp. 185–7*]. The large proportion of freeholders and copyholders by inheritance on many Norfolk manors sometimes made eviction difficult. Article 21, on the conversion of freehold land to copyhold, clearly refers to one method of circumventing this hazard in establishing a sheep run.

The great emphasis given by the rebels to enhancement of rents is more understandable in the light of Professor Phelps Brown's price index for the Tudor period, measuring the comparative cost year by year of a basketful of consumables such as an ordinary family might use [103]. The years 1451–75, a period of stability in prices, are taken as a base period, with the index for these years as 100. There was rapid inflation during Henry VIII's reign, caused at least partially by his currency debasements and military expeditions; by 1548 the index had climbed to 193 and during the years 1548 and 1549 it rose sharply again to 262 in 1550. As prices went up so did rents. The Norfolk rebels had some reason to look back to the 1480s as a golden age before inflation and rackrenting began [*Doc. 17, articles 5, 6, 14 and 17*]. In the 1540s landlords tried to pass on as many of their financial obligations as possible. Among these were payments to the crown or superior landlords for lands held of them, referred to in article 2, and such traditional dues, taking their origin in medieval obligations of military service, as 'castillward rent' (article 9).

Rackrenting was certainly felt to be a major and long-standing grievance in Norfolk, but there is insufficient evidence to be sure whether rents were ahead of, or merely keeping up with, prices. The figures for the Herbert estates in Wiltshire show that rents per acre on new takings increased more than fivefold in the sixteenth century and it has been suggested that the Herbert rent index 'may be taken as generally applicable to lowland England' [75 *p. 226*]. If this is so it would appear that Norfolk landlords had no difficulty in keeping pace with such increased expenses as they had to meet; and where landlords were harsh, their tenants undoubtedly suffered hardship.

The discontents that made up the rebel programme were very diverse. Some, such as the request for fishing rights in article 19, were of purely local significance. This was fulfilled in a grant by charter of all fishes royal, as porpoises, grampuses and whales reserved to the crown by prerogative were called, made by Elizabeth to Yarmouth in 1559. The rebellion provided an opportunity to pursue long-established conflicts in local politics. The corporation of Orford had been at odds for many years with Lord Willoughby of Parham, who claimed that Orford was his seigneurial borough. In July 1549 the leading townsmen, who maintained that a medieval royal charter gave them effective independence, carted Willoughby's bailiff off to Melton gaol to the sound of a drum. They had previously kept him in the Orford stocks for three days and nights. Not surprisingly, Willoughby was prominent in the expeditionary force which defeated Kett [84 *pp. 50–1*].

A more exalted political ghost haunted the Norfolk stirs. No other article in Kett's manifesto has puzzled historians as much as article 16: the request that 'all bonde men may be made ffre for god made all ffre with his precious blode sheddyng'. The clue to understanding it lies in the political situation in East Anglia after the fall of the house of Howard in 1547. The attainder of the third Howard Duke of Norfolk in that year brought to an end a long period of family supremacy. 'The East Anglian risings of 1549 were a popular response to, even a celebration of, the overthrow of the Howard sway' [84 *p. 58*]. Highly conservative landlords, the Howards had retained bondage on such estates as Earsham, Kenninghall and Bressingham in Norfolk and at Earl Soham, Framlingham, Kelsale, Peasenhall and Walton in Suffolk. Soon after their master's downfall, bondmen on four of those Suffolk manors had joined in a petition to Protector Somerset for manumission. One of the reasons that they claimed freedom was 'the charitee of Christe'. They also declared that the third duke had used 'muche more extremitie than his auncestoures did' towards them. The Howards' late headquarters at Kenninghall Park, in an area of south Norfolk from which the rebels drew much strength, had its fences destroyed. Richard Wharton, who was given such a rough passage at Mousehold

Heath, had long been deeply hated locally for his repressive rule as the Howards' bailiff of their lordship of Bungay and Earsham.

No rebellion which rejoiced at the downfall of the Howards was likely to have much sympathy for the old religion of which the third duke had been such a champion. There is evidence for the involvement of traditionalist priests in the Oxfordshire commotions on the far western edge of the 1549 south-eastern movement, but nothing to match the central role of similar clergy in the Western Rising. In Norfolk, some connections with traditionalist religion may be noted: Kett's ties to Wymondham Abbey; his negotiations and personal links with the conservative Bishop of Norwich, William Rugge, and with the devious national and local politician Sir Richard Southwell. These involvements were sufficient to bring Rugge's forced resignation in 1550 and Southwell's disgrace. Other religious conservatives, like the Lady Mary, with her base at Kenninghall Palace, also tried to get involved [84 *pp. 60–1*; 88 *pp. 437, 451–2, 456*]. However, these were probably efforts to jump on a bandwagon rather than a fundamental element of the stirs.

The seven articles in Kett's manifesto which may be classified as religious show that he was constructive in his attitude to the clergy and in his serious concern for their competence. In fact, his thinking on the role of the clergy in society followed the mainstream of the English Reformation. The complaint in article 15 that priests preferred the comfort of residing in aristocratic households to the simple living of the average benefice, and the dislike of their grasping attitude to tithes, expressed in article 22, echo the grievances of the parliament of 1529. The insistence that richer clerics had a duty to 'teche pore mens chyldren of ther paryshe the boke called the cathakysme and the prymer' (article 20) was in line with Cromwell's injunctions of 1536. The idea that preaching was the essential qualification for the ministry (article 8) reiterated Cromwell's emphasis on the need for quarterly sermons in his injunctions of 1538. More importantly, it looked forward to the popular Protestantism of Elizabeth's reign when the 'godly' showed themselves critical of the quality of their clergy and willing to take the initiative in seeking out ministers who were educated and regular preachers. But in this article, Kett made a much more revolutionary suggestion. When a non-preaching minister was replaced 'the parisheners there' might choose another. In this idea we may distinguish an early indication that 'the character of popular Protestantism inevitably tended towards congregational independency' [29 *p. 229*].

Clerical involvement in the active Norfolk land market (article 4) may have been a particularly sore local grievance at a time when beneficed clergy, who could afford it, were offered tempting chances of increased wealth and therefore comfort. Robert Ullathorne of Stockton, for instance, was continually acquiring land in his village between 1543 and 1555 and died in possession of the greater part of the manor of Geldeston [56]. Kett was also aware of the continuing and growing problem of the exploitation of the economic foundations of the Church by the gentry (articles 26 and 15).

There is no question of the Protestant tone of the Mousehold camp. Thomas Conyers, a Norwich incumbent, daily used the new Prayer Book, which had only been officially in use a few weeks, at the services held at the Oak of Reformation. A succession of local evangelical star preachers officiated at Mousehold, including Dr John Barrett and Robert Watson (who was a servant of Archbishop Cranmer), and we know that Cranmer also sent his preachers to the Kentish camps. Revealing was the case of Matthew Parker, a leading evangelical Cambridge don later to be Queen Elizabeth's first Archbishop of Canterbury. Parker's message of submission did not go down well at Mousehold, but he was able to escape when the mood turned ugly. Conyers called on his attendant church choir to sing the *Te Deum* in English: the crowd's delight at this religious novelty diverted their attention from Parker! [77 *pp. 75–6*].

Norfolk had a longstanding heretical tradition: Lollards there in Henry VI's reign had tended towards the more radical forms of belief and there were several heresy cases in the early sixteenth century, leading to three burnings in the years 1507–11 [127]. Now Lollardy was fusing with the new evangelical movement to produce a vigorous popular Protestantism. This was a real problem for the evangelical government clique surrounding Cranmer and the Duke of Somerset: they could not treat the commotions of south-east England with the same blanket hostility which they showed to the westerners. So evangelical preachers were sent in to talk the rebels round, and Robert Watson played his curiously prominent role in the Norwich camp. So Somerset negotiated with Latimer 'the Commonwealth of Kent' and gave him substantial sums of money. This very rhetoric of 'commonwealth' was part of the government's embarrassment. As the Kentish commotion's use of the label proclaimed, it was a traditional theme in popular rebellions; we have already heard it in the 1536 'Pilgrimage of Grace for the common-wealth'. But from the 1530s, 'commonwealth' was at the centre of the reformist jargon which was so freely heard in the entourage of

Thomas Cromwell and then among the evangelical chattering classes who were patronized by Somerset. The commons had made the connection between evangelical religious reform and social reform which had also been made in the Cromwell and Somerset circles, and it is likely that they were aware of this coincidence. John Cheke might sneer at the Norfolk rebels in *The Hurt of Sedition* because 'ye pretend a commonwealth', but he also had to admit that the rebels said that they rose for 'religion', by which they meant the same evangelical faith which he himself professed.

It was easy for government propagandists like Cheke to show scorn for the East Anglian protesters of 1549. But this massive demonstration against the local governing class, based firmly on a mixture of social, economic and religious discontents, was coherent and well organized. The shrill denunciations by the government's publicists reveal its alarm that people outside the magisterial class were able to sustain such an effective protest. The government's final answer in Norfolk, where the rising showed its most determined face, was brute force.

# 7 WYATT'S REBELLION

## CONSPIRACY AND REBELLION: NOVEMBER 1553–FEBRUARY 1554

On 16 November 1553, the House of Commons petitioned Queen Mary to marry within the realm. In her reply she made it clear that she was determined to stand by her decision to marry Philip of Spain. A conspiracy was then formed by a group of gentry who aimed to persuade Elizabeth to marry Edward Courtenay, a weak and unstable man who was a great-grandson of Edward IV. The intention was to put her on the throne in Mary's place. With sufficient support among the nobility and at Court, a political coup might have achieved this. When it was obvious that the Privy Council had accepted Mary's decision, plans were made at the end of the year for a national and popular rising. The leading conspirators were William Thomas, former clerk of the Council to Edward VI, Sir James Croft, Sir Peter Carew and Sir Thomas Wyatt. The three knights had served Henry VIII in his French campaigns in the 1540s. Wyatt had been a member of the English Council in France and Croft had been Lord Deputy of Ireland in 1551–52. Carew, having acted for Somerset against the western rebels in 1549, had sat in Edward VI's parliament as knight of the shire for Devon in 1553.

The rising was planned to take place on 18 March, just before Philip was due to start for England. The French were to provide naval support in the Channel and secure the south-western ports against the Spanish. Wyatt would hold the south-east against imperialist intervention from the Netherlands. A fourfold rising consisting of Croft from Herefordshire, Carew from Devon, Wyatt from Kent and the Duke of Suffolk from Leicestershire would converge on London.

The success of the rising depended on secrecy. In the counties it also depended on the energy and enthusiasm the gentry could inspire in the commons for a nebulous political cause. It was midwinter, the worst time to stir people from their homes, and there was no economic crisis to force them on to the road. Prices were much steadier than they had been in 1549. But scattered pieces of evidence suggest that in the West Country at least there was spontaneous local feeling against the arrival of Philip. This seems to have sprung from wild rumours of Spanish intentions towards the country. At Christmas the French Ambassador heard that Plymouth was preparing to resist a Spanish landing. John Cowlyn, a Cornishman, had heard the rumour that 'before New Year's Day outlandish men will come upon our lands, for there be some at Plymouth already'.

In early January news of the conspiracy was leaking out. Simon Renard, the imperial ambassador and leader of the Spanish faction, knew of it. He was suspicious of the failure of Carew to appear before the Council when summoned, and told the queen as much as he knew. The conspirators hoped to retain the initiative by acting at once. Wyatt had left the capital when, on 21 January, Gardiner, the Lord Chancellor, managed to worm the gist of the plot out of the foolish and unreliable Courtenay.

Abortive risings followed in the west and the midlands. Croft, caught out by the speed with which events had moved, never attempted to raise Herefordshire. The Duke of Suffolk found little support for his cause at Leicester where, in Holinshed's words, 'few there were that would willingly hearken' to his proclamation against the Spanish marriage. Leicester was apathetic; Coventry was hostile. Holinshed relates how the people there 'had put themselves in armour and made all provision they could to defend the city against the said Duke'. When Suffolk heard this news he gave up. He went into hiding but was found and arrested two days later by the Earl of Huntingdon, whom the government had sent north after him. He was escorted to London by the Earl and 300 horse. It was only a week since Suffolk had left London and he had never gathered round him more than about 140 men, most of whom were his own retainers.

Sir Peter Carew had reached his Devon home before Christmas and, in his anxiety to raise support for his cause, made little effort to conceal his plans. His anti-Spanish propaganda gained him the help of a few Protestant gentry but no group of substantial and influential men joined him. For the most part he seems merely to have caused rumour and alarm. The sheriff, Sir Thomas Denys, was determined to safeguard the county from rebellion and retained the confidence of most of the gentry. Carew lacked sufficient influence to carry the county behind him. The commons remembered too well his suppression of the 1549 rebellion. The Devon gentry had mostly acted with the government in 1549 and were associated in the popular mind with the Protestant regimes of Somerset and Northumberland.

So it was Carew's own servants who paraded a wagon-load of armour through Exeter and prepared to defend his manor at Mohun's Ottery, near Honiton. Meanwhile Sir Thomas Denys was active in garrisoning Exeter against attack. Carew began to see that with such insubstantial support his chances of seizing and holding the county town as a demonstration, or organizing a force to march on London, were very small. He became convinced he was about to be arrested and on 25 January abandoned the rising and sailed for the safety of Normandy. The rising in the west had failed before Wyatt had even assembled his army at Rochester.

The crown always had reason to be sensitive to the rise of powerful families in Kent, strategically placed as it was between London and the continent. Partly for reasons of security, it tended to reward its servants and administrators with lands there. Sir Thomas Wyatt came of a family who had served the first two Tudors loyally. The estates he inherited in 1542 made him one of Kent's largest landowners. He was well placed to act as a local leader since from 1550, when he was sheriff of the county, he had taken a particular interest in the defence of Kent and of the Edwardian regime against disorder and unrest. Wyatt took a keen interest in military matters; alarmed by the rebellions of 1549, he had drawn up a scheme to protect the government in time of crisis by a handpicked militia [Doc. 20]. His leadership helped to collect a force quickly when the need arose in January 1554. His success, compared with the dismal failure of Carew and Suffolk, was remarkable. Arriving home at Allington Castle, near Maidstone, on 19 January he spent the next few days coordinating his plans with the small group of his friends whose help he knew he could count on. The government was uncertain of the connection between the news they heard of unrest in Devon and in Kent, but they were bound to treat as serious a threat so near the capital, when there was no army to defend it. They sent a herald to Allington with an offer of negotiations, though there was never a chance of Mary meeting the rebels' grievances. Wyatt dismissed him. On 25 January he raised his standard at Maidstone and proclamations were simultaneously issued there and in other towns. Wyatt then set up his headquarters at Rochester, where by 27 January he had collected a force of around 2,000. Further forces had gathered at Tonbridge and Sevenoaks. It was then only just over a week since Wyatt had come home.

John Proctor relates how the rebel leader went about his highly effective anti-Spanish propaganda. His main theme was the immediate danger to the realm of Spanish control. He dramatized the arrival a few weeks before of the emperor's envoys for the marriage treaty:

> lo, now even at hand Spaniards be now already arrived at Dover, at one passage to the number of a hundred, passing upward to London, in companies of ten, four and six, with harness, harquebuses, and morions, with matchlight, the foremost company where of be already at Rochester.

Wyatt appealed to patriotism. 'Because you be our friends and because you be Englishmen that you will join with us, as we will with you unto death, in this behalf protesting unto you before God ... we seek no harm to the Queen, but better counsel and councillors.' Like other rebel leaders, Wyatt allayed the fears and consciences of many by posing as the rescuer of the queen from foolish advice. He concealed from the majority that he aimed at the deposition of the queen; Proctor claims that when he revealed his true intentions at Rochester to those of his captains who were not already in his confidence, some of them 'wished themselves under the earth for being so unhappy as to be so much as acquainted with so damnable an enterprise'.

But by then Wyatt's propaganda had been sufficiently decisive to ensure that many of the gentry who did not join the rebels at least sympathized with them sufficiently to be unwilling to oppose them. In these circumstances the most active royalists, Sir Robert Southwell, the sheriff, and Lord Bergavenny, found it difficult to raise forces in the county. On 28 January they took up a position at Malling with about 600 men. Here they were well placed to intercept Sir Henry Isley, who set out that day from Sevenoaks to join Wyatt at Rochester. Isley had about 500 men. The two forces met near Wrotham and after a fierce skirmish Isley's men fled the field, leaving the sheriff sixty prisoners. The news of this setback reached Wyatt about the same time that he heard that the royal force of Whitecoats, consisting of 500 hastily mustered Londoners under the Duke of Norfolk, had arrived at Gravesend. Norfolk was now over eighty and past his prime as a military leader. He failed to make contact with Southwell and ignored warnings from Lord Cobham, who had collected 300 loyalists to join him at Gravesend, that the Londoners were not trustworthy. Their disloyalty was dramatically proved when they came down the hill to Rochester shouting 'We are all Englishmen'; according to a pre-arranged plan, they deserted to the rebels. Norfolk retreated to London and the Tower chronicler describes the tattered arrival of his few remaining men: 'You should have seen some of the guard come home, their coats turned and all ruined, without arrows or string in their bow, or sword, in very strange wise.'

Wyatt now had a magnificent opportunity. He had been able to seize some of the queen's ships, ready in the river below Gravesend for the escort of her bridegroom, and some cannon as well. His forces had grown to about 3,000 and the Whitecoats urged him to make a rapid advance: 'London', they said, 'longed sore for their coming.' Everything now depended on the attitude of the city and this still lay in the balance. The Whitecoats' desertion suggested that Wyatt had a real chance of gaining the sympathy and active support of the capital. But he moved too slowly. Leaving Rochester on 30 January he wasted time in an assault on Lord Cobham at Cooling Castle. Cobham was captured and a day lost. On the 31st the government repeated their offer to Wyatt. The Council had rejected Renard's suggestion of an appeal for troops to the emperor and the queen still had no adequate military forces. The queen played for time by offering a committee to discuss grievances arising out of the marriage settlement and a pardon to all those who returned home at once. The ploy worked in that Wyatt was delayed at Blackheath. When, in his reply, he demanded the custody of the Tower and the queen as a hostage as security for an agreement, any chance of peaceful settlement was finally ended.

Mary rose to the occasion. Proclaiming Wyatt and his company 'rank traitors' she made a rousing appeal for loyalty to the citizens of London. She was convinced that her enemies must be heretics; that, as she told them, 'the matter of the marriage seemed to be but a Spanish cloak to cover their pretended purpose against our religion'. She was unscrupulous in claiming that she would follow parliament's advice on her marriage. Then she appealed to their hearts: 'Certainly if a prince and governor may as naturally and earnestly love her subjects as the mother doth love the child, then assure yourselves that I, being your lady and mistress, do as earnestly and tenderly love and favour you.' Here Mary showed some of the Tudor skill in flattery of which her sister Elizabeth was to make such good use. After the cheers and demonstrations of loyalty that followed her speech at Guildhall she felt secure enough to trust herself to the citizens and the forces the Earl of Pembroke was raising, and her determination not to leave the capital grew.

By the time Wyatt arrived at Southwark on the morning of 3 February there were 'men in harness night and day' guarding every gate, and, more importantly, London Bridge was held against the rebels. At Southwark however, as the chronicler relates, the rebels 'were suffered peaceably to enter and the said inhabitants most willingly with their best entertained them'. They waited there three days, uncertain what to do next. Apart from looting the Bishop of Winchester's palace and library, they remained orderly throughout. Wyatt still hoped for support within the city. He realized it was important to maintain a reputation for good behaviour.

On 6 February Wyatt suddenly left Southwark and marched to Kingston. Thirty feet of the bridge there had been broken down but his men rigged it up sufficiently to take them and the cannon across. It was ten o'clock at night when the rebels started their march back along the north bank to surprise the city, still hoping friends might open the gates to them. On the way the carriage of one of the great guns broke down and precious time was lost before Wyatt was persuaded to abandon it. When they reached Knightsbridge before dawn the next morning they were hungry and weary and Lord Clinton's cavalry successfully attacked the main body of the rebel army at St James's Fields. But nearby other government forces put up a craven performance: when Wyatt reached Charing Cross with the remains of his forces, troops nearly a thousand strong under Sir John Gage's command turned tail at the first shots fired against them and scattered to the safety of the gates of Whitehall Palace and the city. There was panic, confusion and misleading reports of defeat in the palace: only Mary seems to have kept her nerve [85 *p. 282; 9 p. 364*].

The Londoners were out early and ready to defend the city, but their behaviour, as Wyatt's dwindling force struggled on up to Ludgate, was strangely unlike the resistance of loyal subjects to a band of rebels. There must have been considerable sympathy for Wyatt and his cause, because it seems likely that the reason why Pembroke's men did not attack until Wyatt was past was that Pembroke could not control them. And some of the citizens lining Fleet Street even drew back to let Wyatt pass [*Doc. 21*]. It may be that the rebels' cries that the queen had granted their requests and pardoned them were believed. As Wyatt approached Ludgate the mood of the populace remained indecisive, but there the gate was closed. He knew then that he was defeated. The people now came down on the side of the government. Some of those who had watched Wyatt advance attacked him as he retreated. The rebel leader soon surrendered and the small band of 300 who had kept with him till the end put up little resistance. About forty people were killed.

The government had survived, but there was no agreement in the Council on a coherent policy of punishment which might ensure the stability of the regime. Mary convinced herself that her fragile victory meant she had the country's support and that it would be strengthened by the return to Rome that she longed for. Gardiner, reading the rebellion along the same religious lines, believed that the only safe course was the extermination of heresy. But Philip, when he arrived, opposed this. Renard pressed the queen to rid herself of Courtenay and Elizabeth, the obvious rallying points for further discontent. He saw no safety for Philip in England with them still alive. Elizabeth was held prisoner in the Tower for some weeks, but no evidence could be found to incriminate her [100 *p. 44*]. In her speech to parliament on the succession in 1566, she made it clear that she had not been ignorant of the practices against her sister, but hinted that she had disapproved of them [101, I *p. 148*].

Mary, as usual, was the victim of confusing advice, but Lord Paget, whose faction had gained considerably in influence from Wyatt's defeat, had the bulk of influential opinion behind him in advocating leniency. No punitive campaign like that of 1536 followed the rebellion. A number of the conspirators were charged with levying war against the queen, but only two were brought to trial. One was acquitted and the other was pardoned after a period of imprisonment.

With public opinion so strongly against severity it was sensible for the government to be lenient. By the end of February about 480 of those who took part in the rebellion had been convicted, but the vast majority were pardoned at once or after a period of imprisonment. Six hundred men who were in custody were brought before the queen 'coupled together two and three, a rope running between them'. After she had pardoned them they were released, to the rejoicing of the city. Less than a hundred executions took place and they were not distributed in an even way to overawe the people of Kent. The Kentish men lost less than thirty out of 350 convicted, eight or nine of whom were gentry. The Londoners suffered more

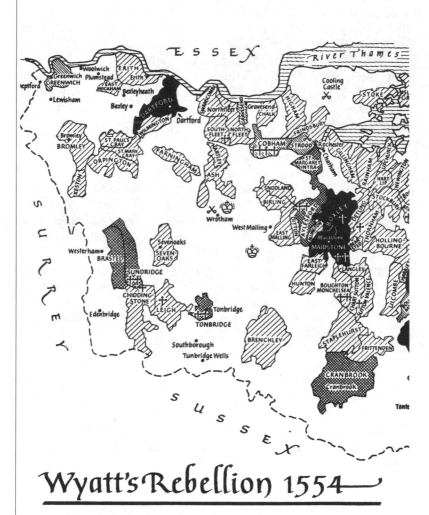

# Wyatt's Rebellion 1554

Map of Kent showing distribution of recorded participants in Wyatt's rising (by parishes). The parishes shown are taken from the first survey of civil parishes, begun in 1838, and approximate closely to the original ecclesiastical parishes.

*Map 4*

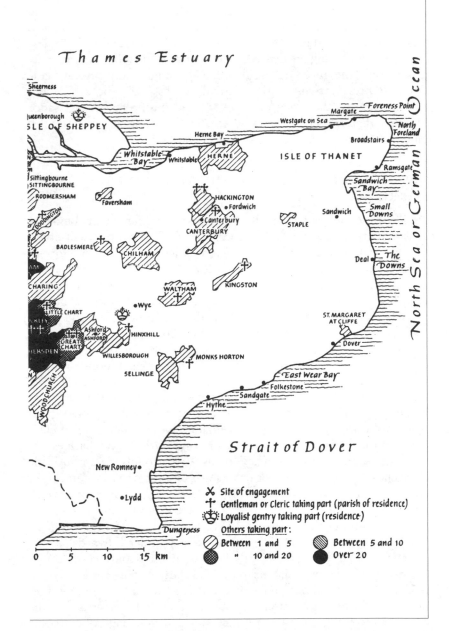

Thames Estuary

Sheerness

Queenborough
ISLE OF SHEPPEY

Sittingbourne
SITTINGBOURNE

RODMERSHAM

Faversham

Whitstable
Bay
Whitstable

HERNE

Herne Bay

Westgate on Sea

Margate

Foreness Point

North
Foreland

Broadstairs

ISLE OF THANET

Ramsgate

HACKINGTON
Fordwich

Canterbury
CANTERBURY

STAPLE

Sandwich

Sandwich
Bay

Small
Downs

BADLESMERE

CHILHAM

Deal

The
Downs

CHARING

WALTHAM

KINGSTON

LITTLE CHART

Wye

Ashford
ASHFORD

GREAT
CHART

HINXHILL

WILLESBOROUGH

MONKS HORTON

ST. MARGARET
AT CLIFFE

Dover

SELLINGE

Hythe

Sandgate

East Wear Bay

Folkestone

Strait of Dover

New Romney

Lydd

Dungeness

North Sea or German Ocean

✗  Site of engagement
✝  Gentleman or Cleric taking part (parish of residence)
👑: Loyalist gentry taking part (residence)
Others taking part:
   Between 1 and 5          Between 5 and 10
      "   10 and 20         Over 20

0    5    10    15 km

heavily, losing forty-five out of the seventy-six convicted. It was perhaps inevitable that the Duke of Suffolk should be executed, and Mary made the decision also to end the lives of the helpless spectators of the affair, Lady Jane Grey and Lord Guildford Dudley. There is conflicting evidence as to whether Suffolk had actually proclaimed Jane queen during the rebellion, but in any case, it made sense to pre-empt any further attempts on Jane's behalf. Wyatt himself went to the block on 11 April and the French Ambassador reported that the people pressed to dip their handkerchiefs in his blood. His legend was quickly being established.

## THE REBELLION, RELIGION AND THE SPANISH MARRIAGE

D.M. Loades argued that 'the real reasons which lay behind the conspiracy were secular and political' [80 *p. 88*]. No one will doubt the political character of the plot: it was led by prominent former members of the Edwardian regime who had done their best to keep Queen Jane on the throne, and who at the very least would not have been sorry to see her back. However, the religious agenda of the rebellion deserves more attention than Loades gave it. It seems curious to overlook the fact that John Ponet, recently deprived Bishop of Winchester and thus one of the most prominent Protestant clergy still at large in England, was among Wyatt's advisers during the rebellion [9 *pp. 363–4*]. It is also deeply symbolic that the only real violence in Southwark was against the property of Bishop Gardiner, Ponet's supplanter and a symbol of all that was traditional in English religion. Not a single prominent figure in the affair can be claimed as having Catholic sympathies.

Of the leading conspirators, Thomas was certainly an enthusiastic evangelical. Carew was notorious as a promoter of Protestantism in the west and was indicted in 1554 '*impie et erronie religionis*'. Croft, the ringleader, had been entrusted with introducing the Protestant liturgy to Ireland in 1551. The Duke of Suffolk and his wife were major patrons of Protestant clergy under Edward VI. The evidence for Sir Thomas Wyatt's Protestantism is only complicated by the considerations that he repudiated any Protestant motive in public for his rebellion, and that the defence of his actions written in the 1590s by an admirer emphasized that 'religion was not the cause of his rising'. Yet this defence came from an age of full-scale war with Spain, and probably exaggerated the patriotic aims of the conspiracy as anti-Spanish propaganda [81; 27 *p. 89*; 128 *pp. 363–73*].

There is evidence of religious radicalism, including anti-trinitarianism, among the Kentish commons in the area around Tonbridge, Maidstone and Cranbrook, and there was certainly a strong mainstream Protestant tradition in Maidstone, where evangelical local notables had seized dominance from traditionalists in Edward's reign. One of the leaders of this group had already gone into exile by 1554 but another, William Smith, a yeoman, was before the Privy Council for distributing heretical literature only a few weeks before the rising took place. Smith himself was among the rebels whose fines were recorded in the Exchequer, and Maidstone provided by far the largest number of recorded participants in the rising. While seventy-eight Maidstone men are recorded, the next largest contingent, Smarden, provided only thirty-two [27 *pp. 76, 91–2*].

The rising in the midlands was ineptly executed and that in the west was inadequately based. Only in Kent was the leadership sufficiently capable to make success possible. As Map 4 (pp. 88–9) showing the recorded participants in the rebellion demonstrates, the strongest contingents came from parishes where there was a gentleman who supported Wyatt. He had the loyalty of a number of influential gentry in the central and western part of the county but hardly any support in the east, which remained largely unaffected by the rebellion. Men like Sir Henry Isley, Sir George Harper and Thomas Culpepper had been closely associated with Wyatt in county government during Edward VI's reign. Successively, these men had been sheriff in the years 1548–52 and a family like the Culpeppers, long established in Kent, enjoyed a network of family connections.

One element in the conspiracy of 1553 to depose the queen was undoubtedly the ineffectiveness of constitutional methods of opposition to the royal marriage policy. Mary was exercising her rightful prerogative when she expressed her annoyance at the commons' petition in November 1553 and told them 'she found it very strange' that they should interfere in such a personal matter; for 'to force her to take a husband who would not be to her liking would be to cause her death'. The rebellion could draw on the agitation against the Spanish marriage that had grown after Mary's intentions became clear earlier in the autumn. Opposition to the marriage was not merely based on fear of foreigners: a powerful motive was the strong suspicion that the marriage would be linked to a restoration to the Church of its lost lands. Catholic landowners could be as worried as Protestants about this.

The rising exploited other fears and rumours of what Philip might do: would he dominate the Court and government and involve the country in the European conflict, with all the heavy expenditure this would entail? The Habsburg grip might be strengthened if there were a child of the marriage, or if childbearing proved fatal. The marriage treaty prepared by the Privy Council and signed on 12 January 1554 in theory safeguarded the country's laws and customs. Only Englishmen were to fill offices in church and state. If Mary died childless, all Philip's rights in England would die with her. But people could not be sure Philip would keep his promises. And in fact when he first heard the terms of the treaty he registered a secret protest that he would not consider himself absolutely bound by them.

Yet there is no evidence that Philip intended through the marriage to try to impose on England a more centralized administration on the Spanish pattern, such as might have weakened or excluded the local power of the gentry, or that he even wanted to rule the country himself. His brief experience of England made him unwilling to come back. The purpose of the marriage from Philip's point of view is more likely to have been primarily dynastic. The Emperor Charles V had been attracted by its diplomatic possibilities in the great struggle of Habsburg and Valois. Its impact on English politics was complicated by Mary's political incompetence. Her distrust of her people was well known, and increased the suspicions of the gentry. Girolamo Soranzo wrote that she scorned to be English and boasted of her Spanish blood.

We lack the evidence to chart the other grievances and discontents which, although irrelevant to the Spanish marriage, may have led particular individuals to follow Wyatt. The largest contingent with no gentry leader came from Cranbrook, the centre of the Wealden cloth industry. Those who were clothworkers may have been more ready to rebel because of unemployment following the depression in the cloth trade since 1551. But it is impossible to impose any pattern of economic causation. Over thirty different trades are represented among the recorded rebels and no one group predominated. Any attempt to explain the rebellion in terms of vested interests, or 'ins' against 'outs', also breaks down. The backgrounds of rebel and royalist gentry were very similar. Both Wyatt and Southwell, for instance, had benefited from the sale of Kentish monastic lands.

The most plausible motivation of those who led Wyatt's rebellion and its associated conspiracies was an attempt to restore the

Protestant ascendancy of the reigns of Edward VI and Jane. Why did the conspirators not publicize this religious and political motivation? For the same reason that the Lady Mary remained silent about the religious theme during the July 1553 *coup d'état* which successfully overturned the reign of Queen Jane. England was a deeply divided country in terms of religion in 1553: it made no sense to limit the appeal of any rebellion by appealing to only one side of the religious divide. It was much better to find a uniting theme, such as the satisfying motif of hating and fearing foreigners, in order to maximize support: hence the concentration on the Spanish marriage. There can be no better proof than Wyatt's own words. 'You may not so much as name religion, for that will withdraw from us the hearts of many', he warned a Protestant supporter. To a doubter who asked 'Sir, is your quarrel only to defend us from overrunning by Strangers?', he replied: 'We mind nothing less than any wise to touch her Grace.'

The foundation of Tudor authority was the dynasty's hold on the confidence of London and the south-east. The Londoners' attitude at Rochester showed that Mary had temporarily lost it. Wyatt came nearer than any other Tudor rebel to toppling a monarch from the throne. Yet in the political development of the century the rebellion's significance is that it failed. This demonstrated the bankruptcy of rebellion as a way of solving this kind of political crisis. The critical issue posed by the Spanish marriage and the succession of a Catholic queen was the question as to who should rule. It appeared that the only sanction, if Mary changed national religion or Philip and Mary broke the terms of the marriage treaty, was rebellion. This was a weapon that, after the social disorders of 1549, few were prepared to risk using. So the gentry learnt to channel their opposition through parliament. They prevented Philip's coronation and frustrated Mary's plans to disinherit Elizabeth by statute. Any plans which Mary cherished to trigger a large-scale return of lands to the Church had to be forgotten. Foreign policy, marriage and religion were all important causes of conflict between Elizabeth and her parliaments; they were also the issues which caused the greatest crisis of Mary's reign.

# 8 THE NORTHERN REBELLION

## CONSPIRACY AND REBELLION 1569-70

The arrival of Mary Queen of Scots in England after her Scottish defeat in 1568 led to a long series of conspiracies. The first complex of these, overlapping in purpose but disconnected, developed in the tense atmosphere of the spring and summer of 1569 when the diplomatic row arising from the seizure of Philip II's bullion ships, a landmark in the breaking of Spanish amity, coincided with a critical situation in Elizabethan Court politics. At the end of a decade of Elizabethan government, Protestantism was not yet secure in its hold on the country and the question of the succession remained open and disturbing. In the intrigues and schemes of this year, it is necessary to disentangle the roles of Mary, and of two groups of nobles – those at Court who disliked the prestige and policies of Cecil, and the Catholic earls in the north.

When Mary crossed the border as a deposed queen she came expecting support in the north. Three years before she had told a Catholic priest that she 'trusted to find many friends when time did serve, especially among those of the old religion'. Among those who paid Court to the exiled queen at Carlisle was Thomas Percy, seventh Percy Earl of Northumberland. During the months of her captivity which followed, Mary exchanged letters with the earl and encouraged his loyalty by sending him and his wife rings and tokens. Northumberland was in sympathy with a group of his friends' efforts to release Mary from South Wingfield Manor in Derbyshire in summer 1569. They failed because of the difficulty of obtaining cooperation within the house.

Mary's future had rapidly become the catalyst of Court politics in 1568-69 [100 *Chs 10, 11*]. The plan for a marriage between the Duke of Norfolk and the Scottish queen made him the central figure in a conspiracy that gained the support of a group of substantial nobility [135 *Chs 8, 9*]. The match was suggested to Norfolk by

Secretary Maitland, one of the Scottish regent Moray's commissioners, at a conference held at York in October 1568 to try to settle Mary's future. It was taken up by Protestants such as the Earl of Leicester and Sir Nicholas Throckmorton, as a sensible solution to two related problems: what to do about Mary and about the succession. By early 1569 it had become part of a Court intrigue to overthrow Cecil, who seemed to more conservative nobles like Arundel and Pembroke to be leading England too close to a confrontation with the Catholic powers. A Norfolk–Mary marriage would enable the queen to settle the succession and make a lasting peace with France and Spain.

But Elizabeth refused to consider letting her leading nobleman marry the most dangerous claimant to her throne. Furthermore, she dealt firmly with Leicester's attack on Cecil for mishandling policy in February 1569. After this, the Court conspirators delayed broaching their plans to Elizabeth throughout the spring and summer because they were afraid of her answer. They hoped that Moray would do it for them as part of the negotiations for Mary's restoration to the Scottish throne. But, late in July, Moray decided against Mary's restoration on any terms. Norfolk spent the summer progress during August in an agony of indecision. He lacked the courage to be open with the queen, who was by now well aware of the rumoured marriage. Finally, on 6 September, Leicester confessed. Ten days later Norfolk found he could bear the atmosphere of suspicion no longer and left the Court without leave. When, afraid to obey Elizabeth's summons to Windsor, the duke then left London for his home at Kenninghall in Norfolk, it was assumed that he had gone to raise the north. Elizabeth, expecting a general rising, quickly took precautions to ensure that Mary's captivity was secure.

There is no evidence that any coherent plan for a rebellion in the north did in fact exist at this stage. Certainly, Mary had been tireless in her letters of encouragement to all whose help she hoped for both in England and abroad. Certainly, the Italian banker Ridolfi had been active in maintaining contact between the southern nobility and the Papacy, and the Spanish Ambassador Guerau de Spes had regularly written to Philip II in wildly optimistic terms about the success of a rebellion. But until almost the last moment the weakest link was the Earl of Northumberland. His resistance to the marriage plan coloured his negotiations with both Mary and de Spes. He had told Mary 'how her marriage with the Duke was disliked he being counted a Protestant, and if she looked to recover her estate, it must be by advancing the Catholic religion'. He had suggested to de Spes that Mary might marry Philip of Spain but had found the ambassador uncommunicative, he suspected 'from my small affection to the Queen of Scots marriage with the Duke'. There is no reason to doubt Northumberland's own account: he was prepared to bring his tenantry to support a Catholic rising but he never intended 'to hazard myself for the marriage' [*Doc. 24*]. The Court conspiracy and the northern rebellion were only tenuously linked; the uncertainty and confusion when Elizabeth outwitted the former provided just sufficient encouragement to activate the latter.

Back in his own country Norfolk's nerve failed him. Instead of raising his East Anglian tenantry and clientage, he spent a week of indecision. He gave no firm lead to the bewildered local gentry. Then, on 1 October, sending a message north to the Earl of Westmorland, his brother-in-law, telling him not to rise, he set out for London to throw himself on Elizabeth's mercy. Within a fortnight he was in the Tower.

That August and September the north had been full of rumours, spread, as Sir George Bowes later reported, 'by the assemble and conference of people at fares'. There were rumours of the Norfolk–Mary marriage and their succession and there was 'the bruit of altering religion'. The earls had read Norfolk's withdrawal from Court as a signal for action and turned from vague scheming to more deliberate planning. The duke's sudden and unexpected capitulation, at the moment when all their hopes had been built on his support and cooperation in the south, forced them to abandon the rising fixed for 6 October. The north was left aroused and confused. News of the abortive rising inevitably reached the Earl of Sussex, who as President of the Council of the North was responsible for the security of the northern counties. The month before the earls and 'all the principal gentlemen and their wives of this country' had been staying with him and hunting at Cawood near York. Though sceptical of the rumours he now heard, he was forced to treat the earls as potential rebels. Sussex knew that because of his friendship with Norfolk his loyalty was already in doubt at Court. In his letters at this time he was anxious to emphasize his activity in enquiring into rumours of sedition.

On 9 October the two earls appeared before the Council of the North at York. They agreed that they had heard the same rumours as Sussex but maintained disingenuously that they did not know their origin. They even said they would 'make diligent enquiry for the first authors'. Sussex accepted their word but reported to the

Privy Council that he had plans ready to take York, Hull, Pontefract and Knaresborough if there were a rebellion. In Yorkshire control of these towns was crucial in an open conflict just as further north control of the country depended on holding the strongholds of such places as Barnard Castle, Brancepeth, Alnwick and Naworth (Map 5). But on 13 October Sussex was confident enough to report 'all is very quiet here and the time of year will shortly cool hot humours'.

Elizabeth was not satisfied about the loyalty of either the earls or Sussex himself. On 24 October she demanded full accounts of the 'bruits' from all the members of the Council of the North; the earls were to be summoned to Court. New and disturbing stories were by now reaching Sussex, that a large meeting was planned at Northumberland's estate at Topcliffe, where he was then staying, and that he would be the first taken. Northumberland himself in fact remained hesitant at this time and had received discouraging replies from Mary and de Spes about the chances of a rebellion succeeding [Doc. 24]. Even the local gentry had 'answered coldly'. But by the first week in November the Neville tenantry were flocking in to the Earl of Westmorland's castle at Brancepeth, while gentry who were determined to remain loyal were gathering round Sir George Bowes at Barnard Castle. Durham was in a turmoil as people suddenly found themselves caught in cross-currents of bastard feudal and national loyalties. Their instinct in such a situation was to move to the safety of towns and castles.

Sussex rightly feared that the summons to the earls would force them into open rebellion, but he had to carry out the queen's commands. Towards midnight on 9 November his messenger, about to leave Topcliffe, heard the church bells ring backwards as the signal to raise the county. Northumberland had been forced into activity by his more enthusiastic followers who made him believe a force had come to take him. He went to Brancepeth where he was persuaded to join the rebellion [Doc. 24].

By 13 November Sussex was sending out commissions for raising forces against the earls. He hoped to collect 1,500 footmen at Darlington by 21 November but he was to be sorely disappointed. Sir George Bowes's almost daily reports to Sussex from Barnard Castle provided a dismal account of the state of the bishopric. It was effectively in the control of the earls and the 300 of their men who had already come in to Brancepeth. Their mounted tenantry terrified the neighbourhood, threatening to spoil any gentry who would not join them: 'They passe in troppes, armed and unarmed, so fast up and down the contrethe that no man dare well stirre anywhere.' Despite all this activity disagreement continued among the leaders and there does not seem even now to have been a clear plan of campaign. On 7 ·November Bowes had written to Sussex: 'Sewre I take this assembly to be more done for fear, than there ys any evil pretendyt to be done.' He continued to think the earls' purpose was more 'theire owne saifety than to annoye'.

On 14 November the earls made their first demonstration, marching to Durham Cathedral where they tore down all evidence of Protestantism and celebrated mass. They returned to Brancepeth for the night but the next day began a march south which they continued till they reached Bramham Moor near Tadcaster a week later. Their progress was slow because they stopped to make proclamations and raise the North Riding on the way [*Doc.* 22]. Durham was the heart of the rebellion: the cathedral had acted as a focus for its emotions and the bishopric provided 794 of the recorded participants. But large numbers also joined the rising from Richmondshire, when their support was demanded with promises of money and under the threat of spoil and burning. Away from their own estates the earls were ready to force the commons to join them. Bowes says that most of the 'poore rascall footemen' were unarmed and 'brought forwards by coercion'. Further additions to the rebels' strength resulted from Christopher Neville's diversion east to raise the Earl of Westmorland's tenants around Kirby Moorside, where he 'threw down the communion board' in the church as the earls had done at Durham.

Sussex, who had only 400 ill-equipped horsemen, dared not leave York and face the rebels in the field. On 16 November he had written bitterly to the Privy Council of his difficulties in levying men: 'Every man seeks to bring as small a force as he can of horsemen and the footmen find fault with the weather.' On 22 November the rebels paused for two days at Bramham Moor. At their musters there they had 3,800 footmen, mostly 'artificers and the meanest sort of husbandmen', and 1,600 horsemen. It was in the horsemen that their real strength lay: they were, according to Bowes, 'for the most part gentlemen and their household servants and tenants and the head husbandmen'.

For a short time the country around York was paralysed by the rebels' presence. A vanguard of horsemen patrolled the Ouse. Sussex stopped sending letters to London for fear they would be intercepted. Lord Hunsdon, coming south to assist Sussex from Newcastle, cautiously approached York by way of Hull. All the country east of the Pennines was at this time at the earl's command.

'All things are here out of order and my dealing and good wyll can not amende yt', wrote Bowes in despair on 23 November. Yet on 24 November the rebels turned back to Knaresborough.

Why did their resolution crack? They may have feared the rumours of the massive force being organized in the south by the Earl of Warwick and the Lord Admiral Clinton or have known that Hunsdon had sent a message warning Cecil to move Mary from Tutbury. However serious they had been in their intention to reach Mary and release her, they now abandoned the plan. It depended on the support of Lancashire and Cheshire and this had not been forthcoming. In fact the appeals that the earls had made to the Catholic nobility had failed completely. Beyond the Aire and the Don was unknown country, a land where the names of Neville and Norton meant little, and a land more firmly linked to the capital by the tentacles of Elizabethan government. At Bramham the rebel leaders realized their weakness outside the north and their nerve failed. As they turned again towards their own estates, the wavering and uncertain country at their backs began to doubt and distrust them. To their north, hope of backing from Scots supporters of Mary was cut off by the resolute action of the Regent Moray, who first forbade Scots participation, and then by mid-December was policing the Border in person with 200 horse [105 *pp. 2–3*].

Once the retreat had begun, the rebels did not stop until they reached Brancepeth on 30 November. Meanwhile Sussex found the tide of loyalty turning in his favour: 'The soldiers wax more trusty', he reported to Cecil on 26 November. He began to speak of the rebels as men with 'their hearts broken'. But a desperate lack of armour and horsemen still detained him in York. The southern army was slow in coming north and with 10,000 men was unnecessarily large and expensive anyway, as Sussex and Hunsdon continually pointed out to Cecil. In vain they pressed the government for 500 horses and 300 shot that they might pursue the rebels, but the Lord Admiral, writing from Lincolnshire, could only offer 100 horsemen.

Although some of the rebel footmen, 'who were promised wages and not paid', deserted and went home on the way through Yorkshire and Durham, 3,200 foot and 1,500 horse came to besiege Sir George Bowes in Barnard Castle in the first week of December. Meanwhile, a contingent went and took Hartlepool, hoping that Spanish troops might land there to help them. But Northumberland later said that the message promising Spanish support was very likely a ruse by Richard Norton, the veteran rebel of 1536, to encourage them. The earls had certainly not maintained regular

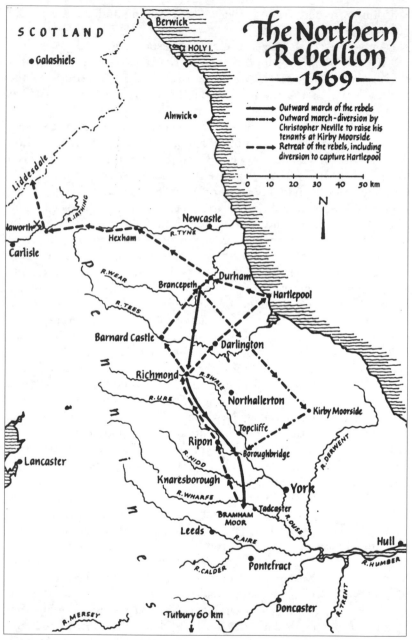

Map 5

contact with any foreign powers. Philip II's attitude in his letters to de Spes had never been more than lukewarm and Alva showed no interest in the conspiracy. The Spanish king was hardly likely to be enthusiastic about a plan to put Mary on the throne, because of her Guise connection.

On 14 December Bowes reported to Cecil how, with the castle near starvation, 226 of his men had leaped the walls to join the rebels. He had been delivered into their hands by another 150 who 'suddenly set open the gate'. The siege was a burst of revenge on the man who had stood most firmly against the rebels in their own country and whose demesnes and crops they had already destroyed. When Bowes surrendered, he was allowed to depart into Yorkshire with 400 men. Yet on 16 December, with the royal army at last near the Tees, the earls disbanded their infantry and fled to Hexham. Here they were approached by the forces of Sir John Forster, the Lord Warden of the East March, coming across from Newcastle. On 19 December there was a skirmish with his scouts. This was the nearest approach to an engagement between the rebel and royal armies. From Hexham the earls, with a smaller body of horsemen, crossed the Pennines to Naworth, the Dacre stronghold. Sussex, Hunsdon and Sir Ralph Sadler reached Hexham (complaining of 'extreme of frost and snow') the day after they had left. Here they spent a bitterly cold Christmas; the earls were first reported to be protected by 'two notable thieves of Liddesdale'. They then fled again across the Scottish border and sought haven among Scots sympathizers, who promptly sold Northumberland to Moray. The pursuers turned their attention to the possibilities of gifts and rewards. Cecil was beset by 'cravers' for the Percy and Neville lands. Only the twenty-year-old Earl of Rutland, who had enthusiastically brought his tenants all the way from Belvoir, seems to have been sorry that the action had never begun. He wrote to Cecil for advice rather than estates: 'I am most willing to serve but all is at an end here.'

The rebellion had failed primarily because of its incoherence and aimlessness, but also because its support remained geographically limited. It had not even mobilized the full resources of the two earls, since Northumberland never had an opportunity to organize the raising of his own tenantry and no more than eighty horsemen came to him on their own initiative. Across the Pennines several vital men failed to stir. Henry Clifford, Earl of Cumberland, was a keen supporter of Mary but lacked vigour at the crucial moment. Leonard Dacre spent much of the autumn in London fighting a lawsuit against Norfolk over the duke's wardship of the Dacre children and his claim to their inheritance. When he returned to the north he fortified Naworth and gathered 3,000 men under the pretence of resisting the rebellion. But by January 1570 his loyalty was under suspicion and Elizabeth ordered his arrest. In February Hunsdon was attacked between Hexham and Carlisle by Dacre but defeated him in a pitched battle; 500 rebels were killed or captured but Dacre himself escaped to Scotland. If he had been at home earlier, the response of Cumberland to the rising in November might have been much more energetic. As it was, Lord Scrope, who had preserved order in Cumberland during the rising, excused his failure to bring troops to Sussex's assistance on 30 November by explaining that the county had 'for a few days stood in great peril'.

The rebellion was contained through the efforts of a small number of active men like Scrope, Sir Thomas Gargrave, the vice-president of the Council of the North, who held Pontefract and organized the mustering of royal troops in south Yorkshire, and Sir John Forster, who was hard pressed to maintain his hold on Northumberland and the Berwick area. Sussex did everything he could with the resources available to him and cannot be blamed for allowing the rebellion to last five weeks. On 26 November Hunsdon, commending him to Cecil, pointed out that 'yf hys dyllygence and carfulness had not been gret, her Majestye had neyther had Yorke nor Yorksher at thys ower att hyr devocyon and commandment'. Sadler held the same view [Doc. 23].

The rebellion, like the Pilgrimage of Grace before it, had been almost bloodless. Apart from the skirmish between Dacre and Hunsdon, the only loss of life was in the siege of Barnard Castle when five men were killed and some more killed themselves leaping over the walls to desert. The rebels had contented themselves with destroying the barns, crops and cattle of those gentry who would not join them. The bloodshed in the government's orgy of revenge was in marked contrast to the rebels' attitude to their victims. Elizabeth ordered that 700 of the rank and file should be executed by martial law. The evidence is too incomplete for it to be possible to reach a precise estimate of the number of executions actually carried out, but it is clear from the papers of Sir George Bowes, the provost marshal, that the queen's intentions were not fulfilled [90]. For Richmondshire and for eighteen townships of the Darlington ward of County Durham the list of those who were executed has survived as well as the list of those picked by Sussex to suffer. These lists show that Bowes, who found the whole task distasteful, did not adhere to the letter of the Lord President's orders. He was prevented from doing so because, as he explained to Sussex, 'although I have both by day and night caused to search their towns they be wholly fled'. In Darlington ward only twenty-four of the forty-one appointed died. In Richmondshire the proportion was fifty-seven out of 215.

Although there is less evidence about what happened in the rest of Yorkshire, it would not be surprising if many escaped elsewhere, considering that Bowes, urged on by Sussex and the queen, had to carry out his circuit of the whole area affected by the rebellion in three weeks in terrible winter conditions. He complained of his difficulties to Sussex on 8 January: 'The circuit of my commission is great, the several places where the prisoners were taken far distant, the weather extreme and the country (except in the bottom ways) impassable for snow.'

Sussex's letters to the queen about the executions are certainly untrustworthy evidence because, in order to satisfy her drive for severity, he tended to report that they were complete for a particular area before Bowes could possibly have had time to carry out orders which Sussex had himself only just despatched. Bowes later wrote in his general memorandum on the rebellion that he did not know how many executions were carried out in Bywell lordship, Hexhamshire and Northumberland since Sir John Forster was responsible for these areas. But the number condemned in the Marches was anyway small; even if Forster carried out his orders more thoroughly than Bowes, the maximum number of those who suffered by martial law seems to have been about 450.

Sussex noted the aptness of the 'occasion not only to settle all these parts in surety but to frame good government along the whole borders'. The long presidency of the Council of the North by the energetic puritan Earl of Huntingdon from 1572 to 1595 went some way towards doing this [33]. Huntingdon's rule was a reflection of the national triumph of Cecil and his Protestant colleagues, who after the 1568–70 crisis were never seriously challenged in government again. Moreover, the rebellion's defeat had strengthened England's links with Scotland because of the strong backing which the Regent Moray had given to the English authorities. Reacting to Moray's murder in 1570, the English used their pursuit of rebels as an excuse to launch three successful military strikes into Scotland; the main result was to throw Mary's partisans into confusion, and strengthen their Protestant, anti-French opponents. England never thereafter ceded the dominant influence in Scottish politics, which in times past had normally been enjoyed by the French [105]. In particular, the two countries were tied together by the continuing problem of what the English should do with the former Queen of Scots. As John Knox put it to William Cecil about the first two years of Mary's captivity in England: 'If you strike not at the root, the branches that appear to be broken will bud again with greater force.'

A number of the rebel leaders escaped abroad. The Earl of Westmorland, Richard Norton and three of his sons and Thomas Markenfeld reached the Netherlands where they lived as pensioners of Spain. Northumberland was less lucky. The Scots government handed him over to Lord Hunsdon at Berwick in June 1572. He made no attempt to evade the searching questions on his part in the rebellion that Hunsdon put to him [*Doc. 24*]. He was beheaded at York in August 1572. Eight of the leaders captured immediately after the rebellion, including two of the Nortons, had suffered at Tyburn in 1570, but many of the gentry involved had been allowed to purchase their lives by handing over their lands and possessions to the crown: a major concern for Cecil and Sussex was to recoup the expenses of the vast army that had marched north to no purpose.

## THE CAUSES OF THE REBELLION

Too often what happened in the north has been seen as an appendage to the conflicts at Court about the Norfolk marriage proposal. By contrast, David Marcombe and S.E. Taylor, the most recent commentators on the rebellion, emphasize the regional crisis which lay behind it [94; 124]. The ancient northern nobility felt a justifiable insecurity after the successive assaults on their power undertaken by Henry VIII, Edward VI and Elizabeth, assaults whose local agents had been successive bishops of Durham. The latest in this sequence of mitred royal servants was the enthusiastic former exile Protestant James Pilkington, whose low opinion of his flock in Durham diocese was mirrored by the magnates' opinion of him. One can imagine what Nevilles and Percies thought of Pilkington's rhetorical questions in one sermon: 'And to rejoice in ancient blood, what can be more vain? Do we not all come from Adam our earthly father?' [94 *p. 123*].

Pilkington, the inheritor of episcopal powers unique among his fellow-bishops, gathered around him a clique of Protestant senior clergy who were unusually aggressive in their promotion of change and who thus aroused much local fury, particularly because of their fierce assault on religious imagery and church furniture from the past. Their innovations were not simply theological; they sponsored a ruthless legal drive to regain full control of church lands which had been leased out by the older generation of clergy to various local families, usually close relatives or friends. Additionally, Queen Elizabeth put selected trustworthy members of her Protestant courtier circle into positions of power in the north: she had put her cousin, Lord Hunsdon, in charge of Berwick and the East March and had deliberately built up the gentry clientele of Northumberland's rival, Sir John Forster. The significance of this became apparent in the rebellion itself, when the areas controlled by these loyalists failed to provide support for the rising, particularly in Northumberland. Altogether there had been a rapid and formidable assault on local vested interests. The only half-way acceptable interloper was the Earl of Sussex (President of the Council of the North from 1568): rather than defusing the tense situation, his cool attitude towards Protestantism may have encouraged the earls to make their move in 1569.

Northumberland, in his confession, explained how the earls were persuaded that they must rebel or flee [*Doc. 24*]. At Brancepeth he resisted those who were 'earnest to proceed', until he saw he had no alternative but to join them. Francis Norton's account confirms that there was no definite plan until Norfolk's departure from Court, when the north heard of 'the Queen's displeasure towards him and others of the nobility': 'We thought there would be some great stir, which caused us to confer together at divers times.' The earls did not take the initiative in these discussions. When it came to action they were in fact only leaders by virtue of their position as feudal superiors. Northumberland's timidity was commented on by Hunsdon, writing to Cecil, on 26 November: 'He ys very tymerus, and yt ys affyrmde, bothe ment, twyse or thryse, too sybmytt hymselfe, but that hys wyfe beyng the stowter of the too, dothe hasten hym, and yncorage hym to persever.' Neither of the earls had the energy of their wives. The Countess of Northumberland rode with the army through Yorkshire and later proved herself an inveterate plotter with Don John of Austria on behalf of Mary Queen of Scots [*82 p. 225*].

Four men can be identified as the main agitators who instigated the rebellion: Richard Norton, the eighty-one-year-old sheriff of Yorkshire; Christopher Neville; Thomas Markenfeld, Norton's son-in-law; and Dr Nicholas Morton, a Catholic ex-canon of

Canterbury Cathedral who had returned from exile abroad. It was Christopher Neville, Westmorland's uncle, who was largely responsible for securing the young earl's participation in the rising. Bowes emphasized Neville's influence over his nephew in his letters to Sussex. Christopher Neville's motives may have been genuinely religious, but he was of a violent nature anyway. In 1554 he had been involved in a riot with three northern families – the Rokebys, the Bowes and the Wycliffes – at Gatherley Races. The feud was evidently still alive in 1569; while Neville was prominent among the rebels, the heads of all these three families were involved in the defence of Barnard Castle.

There is no doubt that the other three agitators acted from an enthusiastic belief in the Catholic cause. Markenfeld and Morton had gone to the continent earlier in Elizabeth's reign and returned in 1568 fired with the enthusiasm of the Counter-Reformation. Northumberland tells of an interview with Morton, during which he spoke of the need to awake the lethargic north and 'lamented the want of sound Catholic priests to whom he might give authority to reconcile such people as would seek it'. Francis Norton later said that Morton was 'the most earnest mover of the rebellion'; he drove them on by warning them of 'dangers touching our souls and the loss of our country'. Richard Norton, who had worn the badge of the Five Wounds of Christ in the Pilgrimage of Grace, certainly seems to have been influenced by Morton's arguments. Markenfeld answered those who doubted the legitimacy of rising before the promised Papal Bull had been published by maintaining that 'the Queen was excommunicated when she refused to suffer the Pope to send his ambassador to her presence'.

Northumberland felt a deep and passionate concern for his faith [*Doc. 24*]. Sir Thomas Gargrave reported in 1572 that 'at or before his dethe he contynewed obstynate in relygyon' and 'affermyd this realme was in a scysme'. He also had bitter personal grievances against the queen. Northumberland had suffered severely from Elizabeth's reassertion of the policies of her father, aimed at weakening the hold of the great magnate families on the marches. Mary had made him lieutenant-general of the north in 1558, as part of her policy of restoring those ancient noble families which had suffered under her father and half-brother. Elizabeth, by contrast, immediately allowed the earl's commission of lieutenancy to lapse, deprived him of his Wardenship of the Middle March and allowed him no part in the custody of Mary. In 1568 the crown had ignored his claim for compensation over the rights to the copper mine discovered at Newlands on one of his estates. Northumberland had declined in wealth as well as status. In 1562 he had written to the Earl of Pembroke that he was forced to 'humblie request her highnes to disburs unto me a thousand pounds, or more, if it may be conveniently granted . . . otherwise in good faieth I knowe not what shift I shal be able to maik'. The Earl of Westmorland was also suffering from poverty. In 1568 he had to borrow eighty pounds from Sir George Bowes. Yet despite all these grievances the earls were most unwilling to rebel; Northumberland maintained in his confession that he 'was drawn into it per force'.

Many of the gentry involved in the rebellion were retainers of the earls. An analysis of the geography of gentry support for the rising shows that the largest groups came from Brancepeth and Topcliffe, the seats of the Nevilles and Percies, while several gentry came from Raby, the other seat of the Nevilles. The custom under which the sons of northern gentry families served in the households of the great magnates enabled the earls to obtain the support of such men as John Sayer and Marmaduke Redman, servants to Northumberland. Redman's father remained neutral but Sayer's actively assisted Bowes in the defence of Barnard Castle. Both Sadler and Hunsdon comment on the way the rebellion split family loyalties [*Doc. 23*]. The Council of the North mentioned this to the queen: 'Many gentlemen show themselfs ready to serve your Majestie, whose sons and heirs, or other sons, be on the other side.' It seems likely that heads of families were too cautious to risk losing their material possessions in the hope of a return to Catholicism.

The strength of the rebel army lay in their horsemen, who were 'gentlemen and ther household servants and tenants'. Such men joined the earls through bastard feudal allegiance. Tenant loyalty goes some way towards explaining the participation of the commons as well. 'The Erle of Northumberland hathe the keepinge of Myddleham, and steward of Rychmond', wrote Lord Hunsdon to Cecil, 'whereby he hathe nowe a grete part of hys force too serve agaynst the Queen.' The lists of rebels pardoned show that Richmond and Middleham were among the towns which contributed the largest number of the commons. But the appeal to bastard feudal loyalty was insufficient in itself to raise a large army; the rebel leaders resorted to religious propaganda, the offer of wages and the threat of spoil in their recruitment drive. Sir John Forster wrote, on 24 November, that he had just heard that 'the Earls have offered wages of sixteen pence a day to all that will come'. Many undoubtedly joined the rebellion because they feared for their lives and goods. On 17 November Bowes reported to Cecil: 'They have constreined, by force, sundrie to followe them; as the people of Bishopton, tenants of John Conyers, my sonne-in-law . . . they not only forced them to go with them, but compelled the rest of the towne, armed, and unarmed, to go to Darneton.' He told Cecil two days later that 'the people compelled to go against their wills, are all ready to mutiny, and many stealethe away'.

The earls' proclamations consistently emphasized the religious issue [*Doc. 22*]. The official ground of the rebellion was to resist the 'new found religion and heresie' imposed since Elizabeth came to the throne. The earls gave a nationalist as well as a Catholic slant to their propaganda. Sussex wrote to Cecil on 17 November: 'They persuade that their cause of seeking to reform religion is that other princes have determined to do it, and this entering of strangers should be troublesome to the realm, and therefore they seek to do it before their coming.' The proclamations were part of a carefully planned campaign to attract the support of the commons. At the Durham demonstration, Richard Norton led the rebels into the city carrying that emotive symbol of northern discontent, the banner of the Five Wounds of Christ. But Bowes's report of an incident at Darlington on 16 November may reveal the hollowness of this campaign: 'Masse was yesterday at Darnton; and John Swinburn, with a staffe, drove before him the poor folks, to hasten them to hear the same' [82 *p. 227*].

The Earl of Sussex was convinced that the people flocked to the earls because they 'like so well their cause of religion'. But Sussex, unable to leave York, was not in a position to form an accurate impression of the commons' motives. It was natural that a man like Sir Thomas Gargrave, vice-president of the Council of the North, should see the rising in religious terms. He was a convinced Protestant, anxious about the future of his faith in the north. In his account of how the rebellion began he emphasized the failure of the religious settlement to take hold in the north. Sir Ralph Sadler wrote of the deep religious conservatism of the people, gentry and commons alike [*Doc. 23*]. 'The ancient faith still lay like lees at the bottom of men's hearts and if the vessell was ever so little stirred came to the top': this was how he thought the conspirators gained their support.

The Elizabethan religious settlement had made little impact in the north during the 1560s. A study of the York Ecclesiastical Commission has shown that it was merely 'attempting to induce or maintain any form of conformity, however shallow' [5 *p. 38*]. Cecil estimated in 1566 that two-thirds of the northern JPs were Catholic. In November 1568 the Earl of Sussex and his council reported that many churches had had no sermons for years past; it was difficult to get preachers to travel and the ignorance of the people was the main cause of their backwardness in religion. Professor Dickens concluded, from a study of the visitation books for the years 1567–68, that 'there existed no recusant problem in the diocese of York'; but he did find plenty of evidence of vague conservatism and popular uncertainty about giving up long-practised rituals [42 *pp. 163, 166*]. There were cases of the use of holy water, images and candles; in the Vale of York some priests were prepared to defy the government by saying the communion for the dead.

The demonstration which was organized and maintained at Durham during the rebellion over several weeks shows how responsive the people could be to a revival of Catholic ritual and practice; also how willing they were to take revenge on the Protestant clergy who had destroyed potent symbols of local pride like Durham Cathedral's banner of St Cuthbert. A group of determined priests gave a strong lead, gaining control of the cathedral services and openly saying mass to large congregations. William Holmes, one of the leading spirits, claimed that he had authority to reconcile the people to the Church of Rome and pronounced absolution to the kneeling congregation. But the variety of militant Counter-Reformation Catholicism which Holmes represented appealed to the gentry more than to the population at large. Professor Dickens believed from his investigation of early Yorkshire recusancy that the characteristic of northern Catholicism was one of survivalism: withdrawal from the Elizabethan order in favour of something older [42]. The popular Catholicism which Morton and Markenfeld found in the north was habitual and uninformed: 'a set of ingrained observances which defined and gave meaning to the cycle of the week and the seasons of the year, to birth, marriage and death' [16 *p. 39*]. The earls found that religious propaganda alone was not enough because rebellion contradicted such a tradition. Without the element of fear of the unknown, which in the earliest stages of the English Reformation had galvanized the Pilgrimage of Grace, it was a tradition that led to inertia not activity, grudging obedience not resistance.

So secular as well as religious tensions in northern society deserve consideration as the context of this rebellion. It may be that political resentment at the extension of Tudor authority in the north was more important in attracting support to it than hatred of

Protestantism. Bowes was hated not for his religious feelings but for his notorious loyalty. The rebellion has been interpreted as 'the last episode in 500 years of protest by the Highland Zone against the interference of London' [119 *p. 251*]. Yet unlike the Pilgrimage of Grace, the rebellion failed to find a wide basis in society. The gentry and their grievances dominated it; Dr Marcombe comments that 'there were very few truly popular grievances evident in 1569 outside of the religious sphere' [94 *p. 130*]. When Elizabeth summoned the earls to Court she precipitated a crisis in northern society, but the cause of Catholicism proved inadequate to sustain the rising that followed. In the aftermath of the rebellion, there were bitter recriminations against the earls for leading humble people into disaster, feelings expressed in contemporary northern ballads. With the leaders fled abroad or (like Lord Lumley and the Percies) removed from their northern estates, the structure of good lordship and military service based on great aristocratic estates decayed for ever [70 *pp. 78–9*]. The failure of the rebellion, its feebleness and its disorganization, all proved that northern feudalism and particularism could no longer rival Tudor centralization.

# 9 EPILOGUE

The defeat of the northern earls represented a turning-point for the Elizabethan government; afterwards Protestant dominance was not seriously challenged. For twenty years, despite many alarms about Catholic intentions, and genuine Catholic plotting, there was no attempt at rebellion. Yet in the last decade of Elizabeth's life, there were plenty of reasons for her and her ministers to feel anxious. Even the climate seemed to conspire against them, with a run of disastrous harvests resulting in full-scale famine in some regions. The price of food nearly doubled while the real value of wages declined [28 *Chs 1–3*].

This was against a background of much higher government expenditure (and hence much higher taxation) caused by war. During the 1580s England and Spain had drifted into full-scale confrontation: the Armada's defeat in 1588, though immediately trumpeted as a famous victory for Protestant England, was not decisive. When the English went on the attack, they proved as unsuccessful as the Spaniards: witness the failed English raid on Spanish-ruled Portugal in 1589, and the lack of any lasting result from such expensive ventures as the naval raid on Cadiz (1596). At least English military assistance to the United Provinces of the Netherlands helped to contain Spanish armies there; however English intervention in France during 1589–91 was hopelessly mismanaged, and the Spanish defeat by 1598 was thanks to the French themselves.

At Court, the queen was aging and losing her sureness of touch amid her leading politicians' jostlings for power [53 *pp. 1–19*]. She refused to name her successor: the chief contender was Mary Queen of Scots' son, James VI of Scotland, but the Catholic Infanta of Spain also had a claim, at a time when England and Spain were at war. The queen's trusted if occasionally troublesome old friends were dying: the Earl of Leicester in 1588, Francis Walsingham in 1590; Sir Christopher Hatton in 1591. Lord Burghley survived until

1598, but he was old and ill, and he devoted his energy to passing on his power to his equally talented son, Robert Cecil. A new political generation was emerging: members of the Howard family were now reviving their fortunes after the 1569–72 disaster, particularly thanks to Charles, Baron Howard of Effingham, victor against the Armada (he became the first Howard Earl of Nottingham in 1597). Most destabilizing was the emergence of Robert, second Devereux Earl of Essex. He was Leicester's step-son by Lettice Knollys; he had all Leicester's restless intelligence, love of splendour and drive to assert his dominance, without the element of restraint which had in the end made his step-father one of the cornerstones of the queen's regime. He automatically saw the Cecils as enemies who usurped the natural aristocratic government of England, but he also clashed with the rival aristocratic house of Howard [53 *pp. 65–86*].

Both popular economic distress and Court intrigue produced rebellions in 1590s England. Both were tragi-comic in their lack of success. In Oxfordshire in 1596, a carpenter and two millers turned up on a hilltop to march on London, but they were rounded up, tortured and executed [132]. This extreme reaction to an event which was absurdly trivial shows just how nervous the authorities were about their situation. In London in 1601, the Earl of Essex, close to a nervous breakdown and facing financial ruin, gathered up a collection of disaffected gentry and younger noblemen (Southampton, Rutland, Sandys, Cromwell, Mounteagle) and tried to make himself master of London [119 *p. 481*]. Although he failed to win any wider support, this was profoundly serious as the first attempt to challenge government in its capital for nearly half a century. Essex may have been mentally unstable by this time, but he had articulated real anxieties: the Court was widely seen as increasingly corrupt, and Elizabeth was not only keeping silent about the succession, but withholding power from the aristocratic younger generation.

Essex's catastrophe had both immediate and long-term consequences. James VI, who had relied on Essex as his confidant on English affairs, reversed his policy and reconciled himself to Robert Cecil. Essex (who had posed as a Puritan warrior-nobleman, in the mould of his step-father and of his wife's first husband Sir Philip Sidney), had identified himself with the war party in fighting the papist Spaniards and Irish. His conduct severely questioned the wisdom of these policies and gave greater confidence to those (like Cecil) seeking a comprehensive peace. Political instability continued to worry those in government into the opening years of the next reign, surfacing in the complex Catholic-dominated intrigues of the Bye and Main Plots against James I, and culminating in the spectacular failure of Guy Fawkes to destroy parliament in 1605.

Whereas England nevertheless weathered the troubled 1590s without producing major rebellions, the situation was very different in Ireland. This book has been entirely about Tudor England, but the Tudors ruled two realms, which now, in the last years of the dynasty, found their futures inextricably linked because of the major rising staged by Hugh O'Neill, third Earl of Tyrone [83 *Part 5*; 99]. From the moment when Henry VIII had arranged for the 1541 Irish Parliament to proclaim him king instead of Lord of Ireland, the Tudors had a fatefully contrasting choice of policies for their second kingdom. They could cooperate with Irish Gaelic and Anglo-Norman nobility as they did with the nobility of England, or they could begin confrontation and colonization. First colonial efforts in Leix/Offaly were undertaken by Philip and Mary's agents in 1556–58. In view of her Catholicism, this was ironic, because in Elizabeth I's reign, the Irish, who were furious at continuing colonization policies, increasingly allied with Elizabeth's Catholic enemies.

Hugh, Earl of Tyrone was the major power in Ulster, that part of Ireland where English rule was most fictitious and Gaelic culture strongest. Increasingly, despite English efforts to detach him from his background and Anglicize him, he saw the only hope for Ireland as lying in a complete break with the Tudors, with the help of Spain and the Pope. He would lead what was for the first time a truly island-wide campaign against the English presence. He seized the English fort at the Blackwater (Armagh) in February 1595; the English government in Dublin declared him a traitor in June 1595. The English were defeated at the Yellow Ford in 1598; the Tudor regime now realized that it faced a battle for the very survival of its rule in Ireland. Essex achieved his ambition of a spectacular military command by being sent with the almost unprecedented powers of viceroy in 1599, but he destroyed himself as a result. He returned home after making unilateral peace with Tyrone, and his subsequent fearsome row with the queen was the beginning of the road which led him to his own attempted revolt. Instead, Charles Blount, eighth Lord Mountjoy, defeated Tyrone by grim military persistence, ending up by routing a joint Spanish–Irish force far from Ulster at Kinsale in 1601. By then the war had turned into a genocidal conflict, in which English forces saw themselves as fighting a barbaric race who deserved no mercy. By 1603, as the queen lay dying, Mountjoy took Tyrone's surrender. It was the beginning of the end for Gaelic Ireland's political freedom; its leaders, Tyrone and O'Donnell, chief of Tyrconnell, would leave Ireland for ever in 1607. Organized settlement of Protestant English and Scots began in Ulster in 1609.

There was a certain relief in England when Elizabeth died, and even greater relief when it became apparent that James VI would easily succeed to the throne as James I. In fact, as the anxieties of the 1590s faded into history, it became apparent how much had been achieved. The dangers of the decade were in the end overcome. At Court, Essex had self-destructed, for all the continuing fears that his revolt was a symptom of a drift back to fifteenth-century-style aristocratic conflict. Robert Cecil guided the affairs of James's government until his death in 1612, very much as he had done since the mid-1590s. He failed to solve the government's perpetual financial problems, but it took a further century of national upheaval before that happened. For the moment, the Church of England was secure; it had silenced opposition, and was increasingly accepted as the spiritual expression of the Protestant nation-state. Spain had been contained, the Protestant Dutch preserved and France kept out of Spanish hands; these had certainly been the aims of English foreign policy in the 1590s, even if the English could only take partial credit for the actual achievement. Ireland had been cowed; this had terrible consequences for the future, but at the time, it seemed a great reward after years of miserable guerilla warfare. Ireland now became the first English colony; the beginning of a world empire; the first hint that England would be something more than a minor European power. Looking back from new troubles in the reign of James I, the last years of Elizabeth's reign seemed full of dogged achievement, and were soon made golden as part of the myth of Gloriana, standing at the head of a united English Protestant nation.

# PART THREE: ASSESSMENT

## 10 REBELLION AND TUDOR GOVERNMENT

If one describes Tudor rebellions, at first sight it seems strange that anyone bothered to rebel: the record of failure looks so consistent, the odds seem so heavy. However, this ignores the truth of Sir John Harington's maxim:

Treason doth never prosper: what's the reason?
For if it prosper, none dare call it treason.

Successful Tudor rebellions have been ignored precisely because they were successful. There were in fact four. The first was Henry VII's takeover in 1485, the second, the rejection of the Amicable Grant in 1525, the third, the overthrow of Protector Somerset in 1549 and the fourth, Princess Mary's seizure of power in 1553. There is one obvious fact about these successes: they all occurred in the first half of the Tudor age. In fact, Elizabeth I had to face far fewer rebellions than her predecessors, and none of them deflected her from her chosen policies. She bequeathed to her successor King James one of the most trouble-free kingdoms in Europe, which was a pleasant change for James, after forty years of coping with Scotland. What was the secret of Elizabeth's success? Was it in fact thanks to her?

If we try to assess the sequence of Tudor rebellions, we have two questions of success to raise. First, what was the recipe for making a rebellion work? Second, what was the recipe for neutralizing the rebellious instinct? To answer this, we must see that Tudor politics operated on two levels, which we can crudely label the high and the low. It is the interaction between the two which makes the sequence of early Tudor rebellions so complex to unravel, and which we must also seek to understand.

First, high politics: the world of the nobility and gentry: the people who directly advised the king, or even on occasions, became king. The issue here was who would run the country. Particularly in the fifteenth century, this meant that high politics was a peculiarly personal or dynastic business. No great ideological issues separated Lancastrians from Yorkists; what turned their struggles into civil war was the complete incompetence of Henry VI and the regional favouritism and ruthlessness of Richard III. Henry Earl of Richmond's takeover in 1485 was a perfect example of this sort of politics. For all his high words about his just title, it was in fact as shaky as it could be without being non-existent. His victory came, even though his army was tiny, because few aristocrats were willing to fight for Richard. Thereafter, most revolts which he faced were similar pieces of high politicking about which family to put on the throne. His answer was to murder or neutralize as many likely rivals as possible, a policy which his son took up in mid-life. One cannot imagine that a White Rose political programme would have differed much from that of a Tudor, that Stafford or Courtenay would have been a very different king from Henry VIII in the 1520s.

The complication came with the Reformation. Suddenly a real issue was injected into this aristocratic game: the most important issue of all in an age which could hardly conceive of a world without God: how should God be worshipped, and how did one attain to eternal life in his presence? That meant that dynastic murders could double as ideological murders, and Cardinal Reginald Pole could at once be a symbol of defiance to Henry VIII's religious policies and the grandson of the Duke of Clarence, much better descended than Henry. Even so, the third successful rebellion, the overthrow of the Duke of Somerset, was not a Catholic *coup d'état*, even though it came in the aftermath of Henry's Reformation and in the middle of a far more drastic and Protestant reformation. Even the fourth successful rebellion, the *coup d'état* which put Catholic Princess Mary on the throne, carefully avoided the religious theme throughout the whole operation. It is only in the one major rebellion which Elizabeth faced, the rising of the northern earls in 1569, that we find a direct attempt to harness traditional aristocratic power to traditional religion – and it failed. The last rebellion of the age, Essex's effort in February 1601, was a return to classic pure high politics, or at least, a classic parody of them. Essex simply wanted to seize power and influence for himself; there were Catholics among his followers, but that merely reflected the presence of Catholics in any group of foolish and frustrated young gentlemen at the time.

Now low politics. 'Low' is a rather patronizing adjective, but at least it acknowledges that there was a second world of politics, which many Tudor noblemen and gentry would be loth to admit.

Leadership qualities and experience were much more widely distributed in sixteenth-century England than social convention suggested. Conventionally, the people who ran the country were the nobility, higher clergy and gentry, plus a handful of career lawyers and, in the special sphere of towns, great merchants. In fact, at a local level, a good deal of power and responsibility was held by people who were not 'one of us'. England was made up of a few large cities, hundreds of medium-rank and small towns, but thousands of villages. Of these villages, only between a half and one-third could claim a resident gentleman. Otherwise, their leading figures were prosperous farmers, who took their turn as church-wardens, bailiffs, jurors and gildholders. As a piece of shorthand, we can style them yeomen, but they might run businesses as well as farm. Particularly if they were involved in the cloth or the meat trade, they might travel round the country a good deal; they were well-informed, independent-minded, and used to dealing with a wide variety of people, and used to running their own and other people's affairs. These were the people who led popular Tudor rebellions.

Politically astute noblemen were quite aware of this reality; leading yeomen could be seen as a good investment for a rebellion. Take a significant speech of a great magnate gone to the bad, Lord Thomas Seymour; either he actually said these words to the Marquis of Dorset in 1548, or his enemies thought that they could plausibly be put into his mouth as a recipe for his planned rebellion:

> . . . trust not to much to the gentlemen, for they have sumwhat to loose; but I wold rather advise you to make muche of the head yeomen and frankelynes of the cuntreye, speceally those that be the ringeleaders, for they be the men that be best hable to perswade the multitude and may best bring the number; and therefor I would wishe you to make muche of them, and to goo to their houses, nowe to oon and nowe to an other, caryeng with you a flagon or two of wyne, and a pasty of veneson, and to use a familiaritie with them, for soo shall you cause them to love you, and be assured to have them at your commaundement; and this maner, I may tell you, I entende to use meself. [112 *p. 15*]

We can also note that this yeomen class which led rebellions was also the class which provided England with most of its clergy, right up to the bishops. It was therefore likely to be a class much prone to righteous indignation. What were the issues which made yeomen angry? If high politics was about *who* should run the country, low politics was about *how* the country should be run. High taxes, perversion of justice, aristocratic highhandedness, hoarding of food supplies – these were the issues which brought periodic eruptions of fury. Taxation was one of the chief symbols of chronic misgovernment. The Earl of Northumberland was murdered in 1489 when he turned into a royal tax collector. Back in 1381, the same thing had happened to an Archbishop of Canterbury, while the Duke of Suffolk had fallen victim to lynch law in 1450 because he had become the symbol of general misgovernment. However, taxation became an even more bitter issue from the 1520s because Henry VIII was demanding much more money to fight his succession of French wars. Henry made things much worse because as part of his fund-raising, he introduced the most cruel and irresponsible form of indirect taxation possible: debasing the coinage. War and taxation lurked behind practically the whole sequence of mid-Tudor rebellions.

Religion mattered in low politics as well as high during the Reformation. Indeed, it had been a live issue in low politics throughout the fifteenth century, at a time when the gentry had ceased to quarrel about religion. Lollardy took refuge among yeomen when the Lancastrian kings persecuted it out of high politics. As a result, low politics was hospitable to new religious dissidence when it appeared from the continent in the 1520s; this new reformism gradually merged with Lollardy. Some yeoman leaders, however, reacted with horror at the prospect of change in the society in which so many were church and gild wardens, and which meant much to so many in terms of happiness, religious satisfaction and personal status. So in 1549 the world of low politics divided sharply in religious allegiance: the western rebels demanded the withdrawal of the new English Prayer Book while the eastern and home counties rebels happily used the same Prayer Book in their camps. Yet at the same time, both east and west took a stand against what they saw as misgovernment by their social superiors.

Low politics, even the low politics of rebellion, was a world of order. Most rebellions, after all, started as riots, and riots were a constant feature of English life, as much controlled by certain conventions as a violent game of rugby. Yeomen were fully familiar with the courts of law, and devoted a significant part of their spare income to using them. The processes of English common law actually encouraged formalized acts of violence, such as symbolic trespass on land, in order to get a legal case started, while in order to get a grievance into the most effective court in the land, Star Chamber, it was absolutely necessary to construct a riot, which might be collusive between the twó sides just as much as a random piece of angry violence.

What is at first sight surprising in mid-Tudor violence is to find a battle between two individuals scamper between the lawcourt and the rebellion. To adapt Clausewitz, rebellion could be a lawsuit by other means. A cry comes down to us from one of the East Anglian rebel camps of 1549: a merchant confronted a gentleman who had been captured by the rebels as a hostage, and demanded compensation for an old trespass, saying 'Nay, I will have it now, ere I go, or I will complain, for I know I shall have remedy here' [84 *p. 48*]. The same merchant went on to seek 'remedy' elsewhere, for he had the cheek to sue the gentleman for the same compensation in the Court of King's Bench. At Norwich, the 1549 rebels even helped the royal purveyor go about his highly unpopular task of collecting cut-price grain for the royal armies in Scotland.

It is worth remembering the useful generalization of Yves-Marie Bercé: 'The trigger of revolt is not destitution, but injustice – and not objective injustice, but the conviction of it' [11 *p. 221*]. Rebels were seeking to do what was right. The main reason that they were rebelling was that they felt that their social superiors were not doing what was right. In fact most would have hated to be called rebels, and the 1549 'rebels' in eastern England behaved in a very distinctive way when they staged their rebellion. Rather than marching on London as the western rebels did, they formed camps and sat in them; their rebellion became known as 'the camping time'. There is a clear contrast with the urgent movement in the rebellions staged by practitioners of high politics: Henry Tudor's invasion of 1485, Lambert Simnel's invasion of 1487, Mary Tudor's East Anglian coup of 1553. Other Tudor and earlier rebellions display the same lack of mobility as in the 'camping time': the Lincolnshire rebellion of 1470, the events surrounding the assassination of the Earl of Northumberland in 1489, even the Pilgrimage of Grace. In the distress of the 1590s, the suffering poor saw the formation of camps as an end in itself, in places as widely dispersed as Essex, Kent and Norfolk – in order to secure justice [132 *p. 92*].

The point was that camps had an analogy in ordinary times which spoke precisely of justice and remedy. Well into the sixteenth century, many meetings of the assizes nationwide were held in the open air; several camps in 1549 were held in traditional assize centres. One of the reasons that the people rose in 1549 is that they had caught a rhetoric of remedy, reform and social criticism from high politics: the rhetoric of commonwealth, which gave its name to the Kentish section of the stirs. At Norwich, the camp had an Oak of Reformation to dispense justice: an open-air court. The 1549 camps were probably more like a rough and ready garden fête or assize meeting than the savage centres of misrule which the government later tried to picture.

Low politics was a world of order: it was also a world of tradition, which could draw strength in a rising from exploiting well-established patterns of popular protest, just as the Lollards came to express their dissidence over generations in certain communities and certain families [26 *p. 378*]. The recurrence of one village, St Keverne, in Cornish disturbances is quite remarkable, but in any case Cornwall was a culture to itself with a recurrent pattern of independent political behaviour from the fifteenth century to the Civil War [121 *p. 321*]. One notable south-eastern example of a linked pair of communities is from Suffolk: Lavenham and Brent Eleigh. The pairing is especially striking because of their apparently contrasting characters: Lavenham was an important town and a centre of the cloth industry; Brent Eleigh, then as now, was a very small agricultural village. After the protest in 1525 against the Amicable Grant, the two communities were particularly singled out as places where the inhabitants should do penance for their resistance. In 1549 Lavenham and Brent Eleigh gave particularly solid support to the Bury camp. Moreover in 1569, in an abortive East Anglian popular rising, the Lavenham leaders again planned to go to Brent Eleigh to recruit support before they showed their hand [84 *p. 52*]. Many disorders were associated with the traditional rhythms of the year which brought people of a region together to trade, to play and generally feel good – notably the 1549 commotions in the south-east. In 1533 the Imperial Ambassador reported that Henry VIII's government was nervously trying to suppress traditional summer meetings of armed men on St John's and St Peter's Eve; while the vicious riot against foreigners in 1517, the most serious disturbance to start in London all century, is known as Evil May Day. Well into the seventeenth century, Londoners could expect serious trouble on that other great popular holiday, Shrove Tuesday [79 *pp. 109–10*].

It was difficult for the world of high politics to accept that low politics existed, let alone had its own ideas about good government and competent administration. Lord Thomas Seymour saw the reality, but he was an unusually cynical and indiscreet nobleman.

Most of his fellows would not admit what he is alleged to have said in 1548, and the idea of political competence among their inferiors filled them with horror and indignation. Their horror led to a fantasy picture of Tudor rebellions. Repeatedly, the people of later Tudor high politics saw the reality of low-casualty, semi-orderly English commotions in terms of the mad violence which the militant Anabaptists had inflicted on the German city of Münster from 1533.

Faced, for instance, with a remarkably efficient takeover of East Anglia in 1549, the official commentators tried to turn the story of the whole venture into a monstrous rising of crazed wretches, and it was only left to observers on the sidelines to give a more balanced account, like the chronicler in far-off Bristol who described Kett's Norfolk army as 'full of courage and skillful'. In fact during the sixteenth century, popular violence was remarkably restrained compared with the previous century. During the fifteenth century, five English noblemen were murdered by mobs; the only noblemen to die in sixteenth-century rebellions were killed in active combat against rebels. A rare exception to the general rule was an abortive rising at Seamer in Yorkshire against the Edwardian Reformation in 1549. This consisted, according to Foxe, of a plan 'at first rushe to kill and destroy such gentlemen and men of substance about them, as were favourers of the kynges procedynges, or which would resiste them' [41 *p. 33*]. Foxe says that four gentry were taken and murdered: 'After they had strypped them of their clothes and purses, they left them naked behynd them in the playne fields for crowes to feede on' [73 *pp. 452–3*]. Acts of violence against the nobility, such as the killing of Lord Sheffield by Kett's rebels, were useful material to men like Sir John Cheke, employed to paint a picture of traitors who presumed to usurp the political role of their superiors. In general, however, time and again far more acts of violence were committed by the government in reprisals than were ever committed by rebels. So government reaction to rebellions repeatedly revealed the gulf between the two worlds of politics, and the fear which the high had of the low.

It is this gulf which helps us to explain both success in staging rebellions and success in preventing them. It came from bridging the gulf between the two politics. Consider once more a successful rebellion. The lesson of repeated attempts at popular rebellion was that they could not succeed on their own. The second successful Tudor rebellion was the defeat of the Amicable Grant in 1525. The Dukes of Norfolk and Suffolk, the only two dukes in England, were prepared to restore order by ritually humiliating the demonstrators, but they also advised against any actual violence, and they forcefully advised the king and Cardinal Wolsey that the tax should be dropped. This affair was the first major mistake that Wolsey had made in government, and it showed the power of combining popular and aristocratic discontent. Not enough people in power believed in the tax to push for its enforcement, and many of them saw it as the particular idea of a minister whom they disliked and envied. Similarly, in the Pilgrimage of Grace, massive success came to the rebels in autumn 1536 when commons and nobility combined, bringing the government to make humiliating concessions. When mistrust overcame this frail cooperation, the attempts at renewed rebellion by the commons alone in winter 1537 were a fiasco.

A further sequence of eastern risings makes the same point about the necessity of cooperation. The rebellions of eastern and southern England in 1549 were paradoxical, because on the one hand they enthusiastically took up hints that the Duke of Somerset was intending radical reform, and on the other, showed real anger at the local misgovernment of the gentry. This was a rebellion of churchwardens appealing against justices of the peace to the Lord Protector. But the rebels soon found that Somerset was a false friend, interested only in their dispersal, and when things went wrong in Norfolk, in their suppression. The Norfolk folk made no gentry friends, had no one to listen to their grievances. Once they had been bloodily suppressed, the country's leadership staged its own high-political rebellion against Somerset to punish him for his clumsy encouragement of the lower orders.

The next great rising in eastern England, in 1553, was a complete contrast. In it, a group of gentlemen reacted to an eruption of popular anger against the Westminster leadership in order to overthrow Queen Jane and put Henry VIII's daughter on the throne. Ordinary East Anglians flocked to Mary's palace before the gentry did; sailors in a fleet off the Suffolk coast mutinied against their officers. One nobleman of ancient lineage, the sixteenth Earl of Oxford, found himself unceremoniously bundled on to his horse by his own servants to go and swear loyalty to Queen Mary [85 *pp. 214–15, 263–4*]. Faced with this, all over the country local gentry and urban leaderships were forced to do a reverse turn; the leaders of high politics in Westminster did not have enough conviction about what they had done to keep up resistance against both their own kind and against ordinary people. Proclamations of Queen Jane were hastily forgotten and the evidence destroyed. Popular satisfaction at the turn of events was probably heightened in East Anglia because it was a revenge on the Duke of Northumberland for his destruction of Kett's Rebellion; but the victory was a triumph of partnership between high and low politics: a success where similar cooperation in the Pilgrimage of Grace had only narrowly failed.

Equally, to neutralize a rebellion, one must seek a meeting and understanding between the two worlds: create once more the trust which had been lost. If Lord Thomas Seymour recommended pasties and wine for the ringleaders among the yeomen, that combination could be used just as much to stop trouble as to start it. Take once more the 1549 commotions in eastern England. The rising covered Kent, Sussex, the Thames Valley, Cambridgeshire, Suffolk and Norfolk, but most of it was sorted out without a fuss, and only the Norfolk section became a rebellion. The strategy adopted was to choose leading figures at Court who were respected in their home counties to go and talk to the rebels and offer them pardons and money. There are traces of this happening all over the south-east; Lord Wentworth of Suffolk was actually made a Privy Councillor so that he would be more impressive to the rebels back home. In Sussex the Earl of Arundel, a nobleman of the most ancient lineage, stopped trouble by inviting prominent malcontents round to dinner. Only in Norfolk did the scheme go wrong, for the simple reason that there was no one convincing to do the job. The Duke of Norfolk would have been the obvious person in the past, but he had been locked up in the Tower for two years. The government had to send in an outsider, the Marquis of Northampton, and he wrought havoc, involving bitterness, expense and many more deaths. Sir Peter Carew, a similarly unsympathetic figure to the western rebels of 1549 because of his religious views, had a similar effect on the situation in Devon.

Prevention, then, was better than cure when a rebellion broke out. The best prevention was to watch for any build-up of righteous indignation in low politics and use all the resources of the Tudor state to head it off before it got to the point of open demonstration. The government must show that it was responsive, that it could listen; it must also show that it was powerful, and ought to be obeyed. There should be both carrot and stick.

First, the monarch should be seen, and in the best light possible. Monarchs should go on progress, and use all the theatre at their disposal to delight and overawe their subjects. Oddly enough, Henry VIII was bad at using progresses effectively. He usually toured the counties nearest London, and was highly reluctant to go north. That may be one reason why the Pilgrimage of Grace happened; it is interesting to remember the Pilgrimage of Grace which did not happen in 1536, in the highly conservative and prosperous West Country. One reason that the west did not rise may well be that Henry actually stirred himself to visit it in summer 1535. He made a major tour of the west as far as Salisbury and the Bristol Channel. This was an occasion of major royal spectacle and feasting, and it is noticeable that Henry gave particular attention and favour to gentlemen of reforming sympathies. It would have been very difficult for west country people to claim that the government had been seized by a reformist clique without the king knowing, which is what much of the Pilgrims' propaganda said in the north.

It took Henry five more years before he could be persuaded to go to Yorkshire and Lincolnshire, and that was after the small-scale renewal of rebellion by northerners in spring 1541. Even then, the main reason for Henry's going north that summer was his arranging an important diplomatic meeting with the Scottish king at York. James did not turn up, with fateful consequences for Anglo-Scottish relations, but the progress was by no means a waste of time. What is significant is that the king's journey was punctuated by formal and abject apologies in words and cash from the people of Lincolnshire and Yorkshire for their region's participation in the Pilgrimage five years before. Hall's Chronicle records that towns, cities, the 'Parts' of Lincolnshire, gentry and clergy, each made representative gifts as reparations for what they had done. The progress was a symbolic reconciliation of king and country, and it worked; there was virtually no further trouble from the north, even in the religious ferment of Edward VI's reign.

Obviously the progress could only be an occasional asset to government. The state must contain a whole galaxy of what Sir Geoffrey Elton called 'points of contact': government must be seen to be accessible, sympathetic. In the provinces, people must be able to feel that they had access to the king's Court through the great men of their area; they must have confidence in royal courts of justice; they must also be confident that their views would be heard in parliament. Parliamentary representation much increased under the Tudors, both in the number of borough seats and in the area which representation covered. Through the sixteenth century the overall number of commons representatives increased by more than 50 per cent, from around 300 to 462 in 1601.

However, contact by itself was useless if it did not lead to action: the public must feel that it was getting something in return for its complaints. Clearly that happened in 1525, when Wolsey joined in the theatre of reconciliation and sued for pardon for the ringleaders of the demonstration because they came from his native Suffolk. Even in the Pilgrimage of Grace, the public could see results. From a religious point of view, the rebellion was a disaster for the Pilgrims, with the religious world which they tried to defend all the more hastily destroyed; but their grievances on taxation and agricultural levies were heard. At a national level, threatened tax reforms were withdrawn for good, and at a local level, landlords in Cumbria toned down their attempts to get maximum financial advantage from gressums and other customs of tenure [21 *pp. 314–15, 417*]. Gentry worries about the effect of major legal changes affecting their inheritance were accommodated when the 1535/36 Statute of Uses was modified by the Statute of Wills in 1540. In 1549, the Norfolk rebels prayed that 'bondemen may bc made ffre, for god made all ffre with his precious blode sheddyng': scores of them were indeed made free by royal grant over the four years after the rebellion ended [*Doc. 17*]. Moreover, after 1549, Tudor government gave a wide berth to taxes on livestock and excises which had caused such fury in the West Country [22 *p. 397*]. So rebellion could produce results; that showed that the government did listen. This was a difficult and delicate issue, given that public ideology was that rebellion was a blasphemy against God whose only reward could be punishment.

In 1558 Elizabeth I inherited a country which had seen four successful rebellions in seven decades, and which had been seething with disturbances for the entire previous decade. The queen then pushed through a religious settlement which many of her subjects disliked and of which only a minority positively approved. The prospects were gloomy, and there was plenty of continuing minor local trouble; yet in the end, Elizabeth faced only one serious internal challenge, in 1569. Elizabethan and early Stuart lawcourts even came to recognize the lessening violence of the age. After 1569 they had to deal with riot and disorder rather than rebellion, and in response, from the end of the century they evolved a new legal offence to deal with these situations: sedition. The penalties for sedition were serious enough, but did not involve the full savagery of the law of treason. It was a clear acknowledgement that a lesser crime demanded a lesser punishment [92].

Why did the situation change after 1569? First, Elizabeth was better at public theatre than her father. She played up all the rhetoric of obedience to divinely appointed royal power which her predecessors had developed. Famously, she built up an image of herself which even included appropriating some of the verbal imagery associated with the Blessed Virgin Mary [54]. This was helped by the accidents of international politics. The Protestant cause of Elizabeth's regime increasingly stood out against foreign Catholic great powers and a Pope who had actually ordered her own Catholic subjects to kill her. Although a handful tried, and failed, nearly all Catholics were as horrified as Protestants at the idea. The deep loyalty to the children of Henry VIII which had served Mary well in 1553 and 1554 became all the stronger towards Elizabeth.

Elizabethan national loyalty was also strengthened by the government's cowardice. After all the debate and argument about the Tudor revolution in government, we can be safe in seeing the first half of the sixteenth century as an age of enormous change in English society and government: obviously at the religious level, but also in the way that England was governed both locally and centrally. Those changes could have been even more sweeping, but Elizabeth's government gave them up. Above all, Elizabeth failed to tackle the most vital and the most dangerous area of English government: taxation. Henry VIII had made many efforts to reform England's antiquated tax system, and most of them failed. Above all, he failed to convince English people that taxation should be a normal part of their peacetime lives, that it was not an unpleasant extra forced on them when England was at war. Elizabeth did no better. In administrative change, she was a complete coward. The actual amount of the subsidy fell: the real value fell even more sharply, undercut by inflation. The assessment of the wealthy became a 'farce' [115 *p. 254*], and the burden fell increasingly and disproportionately on the middling and the poor. By not dealing with these problems, she avoided facing an Amicable Grant demonstration or the tax grievances of the Pilgrimage of Grace, but she also left a huge problem for her Stuart successors to sort out.

National loyalty was also strengthened by the fact of the government's success against the 1569 rising. If any challenge could have brought down the Elizabethan Protestant regime, it was this: the perfect combination of aristocratic power and conservative religion which had also made the Pilgrimage of Grace so potentially dangerous. The reasons for its failure lay in a combination of irresolution, hopeless planning and changing times. The 1569 failure showed that the Tudors had persuaded enough people even in the remote north that the most important political loyalty in their lives was to the crown and the central government at Westminster. Even in the desperate 1590s, Elizabeth faced only two risings in England: one from low politics, one from high politics. The efforts of the pathetic Oxfordshire conspirators and the Earl of Essex proved to be a far cry from Bosworth Field, or indeed from Naseby.

Nevertheless, can the Elizabethan regime take all the credit, both negative and positive, for the decline in rebellions in Tudor England? There is a wider explanation, which takes us back to low politics. We have seen the sort of people who led rebellions. These 'yeomen' sustained the Lollards, marched to Lavenham to shout down the Amicable Grant, became the captains of the 1536 and the 1549 risings. They would remain part of the complacent English myth of self-identity, as in the military regiments who in this century still proudly called themselves the Yeomanry. But yeomen changed during the sixteenth century. Their world came closer to that of their gentry superiors, and in one particular respect: literacy. By the 1580s, for instance, David Cressy's findings are that in the diocese of Exeter yeoman illiteracy had fallen from 75 per cent to 35 per cent in the previous thirty years, and in the diocese of Norwich, from about 60 per cent to about 30 per cent [32 *pp. 162–68*]. From then on, a majority of the middling sort of craftsmen and small farmers, even in small villages, were literate, the result of increased schooling in mid-century. At the same time, their social inferiors, the husbandmen and labourers, remained steadily illiterate at between 75 per cent and 100 per cent right up to the nineteenth century.

Thus, in the reign of Elizabeth the yeomen leadership of low politics was becoming closer to the gentry than to the class below. Literate culture was the culture of the powerful. Yeoman society began taking on the ways of the world of power; for instance, the inventories of their possessions on their deaths and their wills reveal musical instruments like virginals in their homes. Many of them took with enthusiasm to the new respectable activism of Puritan religion. They were less inclined to use violence to express their anger; they would take their grievances to the royal lawcourts, and turn up in their hundreds or even thousands to vote in county elections to parliament. There might be plenty of excitement and brawling on an Elizabethan election day, but it was a far cry from the slaughter of Kett's army on Mousehold Heath.

So the emphasis in the conflicts of low politics moved from direct action in the countryside to alternative arenas – the lawcourts, the high court of parliament. These were traditional arenas, but all the more effective because of that in siphoning off popular protest. Each embodied the majesty of the law: and Tudor low politics showed perhaps even more respect than high politics for law and justice. It would take Charles I to unlearn all the lessons that his Tudor predecessors had learnt from their rebellions: to combine the leaders of high and low politics once more in open violence against the English state.

# PART FOUR: DOCUMENTS

TRANSCRIPTION

In these extracts the spelling and punctuation follow the source used. Words in brackets are conjectural interpretations where a manuscript is torn or unreadable.

## DOCUMENT 1    THE DUKE OF NORFOLK TO WOLSEY, 1525

*The Duke of Norfolk made this report from Lavenham on 11 May 1525. The gathering of the Suffolk commons was the nearest approach by those who resisted the Amicable Grant to open rebellion.*

Pleas it your grace to bee advertised that this day at x a clock we the Dukes of Norfolk and Suffolk mett to gethers at a place appoyntid ii myles on this syde Bury with all the company of bothe the shires whiche was a right goodly company to loke upon at the leste iiii thousand whiche were gatherd sithins Tuisday in the mornyng. And unto us cam the inhabitauntes of the towne of Lavenham and Brant Ely whiche were offenders to a great nombre. They cam all in theire shirttes and kneling before us with pitious crying for mercy shewed that they were the kinges moste humble and faithefull subgiettes and soo wold contynu during theire lyves saying that this offence by them comitted was only for lack of worke soo that they knewe not howe to gett theire lyvinge. And for theire offence moste humbly besought us to bee meanes to the kinges highnes for pardon and remission, unto whome we made a long rehersall the beste we coulde to agravate theire heynous offence declaring the same to be highe treason and laying the soreste we could to theire charges as well of their evell demeanour againste the kinges highnes as of theire rayling wordes. Finally we tryed out iiii of the pryncipall of the offenders ... we gave all the reste leave to departe save thouse iiii with as sharp and sore lessons any more to do like offence as we could devyce.

B.L. Cotton MSS, Cleopatra F.VI. fol. 325; *Letters and Papers of Henry VIII*, iv (1) 1323.

DOCUMENT 2    THE EXAMINATION OF NICHOLAS
LECHE, 1536

*Nicholas Leche, the priest of Belchford, took the initiative in raising the*
*commons around Horncastle. He was tried for treason and executed at*
*Tyburn in March 1537. His examination throws interesting light on the*
*cooperation of the gentry and commons in Lincolnshire but it should be*
*treated with caution since it is likely that Leche did his utmost to dissociate*
*himself from the leadership of the rising.*

The gentlemen were always together commonly a mile from the commons.
What they did he knows not, but at length they brought forth certain
articles of their griefs, of which one was that the King should remit the
subsidy, and another he should let the abbeys stand, which articles George
Stanes openly proclaimed in the field, and the sheriff and he, about
Langwith field, said to the commons, 'Masters ye see that in all the time we
have been absent from you we have not been idle. How like you these
articles? If they please you say Yea. If not, ye shall have them amended.'
The commons then held up their hands and said with a loud voice, 'We like
them very well.'

Amongst other articles there declared, Mr Sheriff and other gentlemen
said, 'Masters, there is a statute made whereby all persons be restrained to
make their wills upon their lands, for now the eldest son must have all his
father's lands, and no person to the payment of his debt, neither to the
advancement of his daughter's marriages, can do nothing with their lands,
nor cannot give his youngest son any lands.' Before this he thinks that the
commons knew not what the Act of Uses meant. Nevertheless, when that
article was read to them, they agreed to it as to all other articles devised by
the gentlemen. He thinks all the exterior acts of the gentlemen amongst the
commons were done willingly, for he saw them as diligent to set forward
every matter as the commons were. And further, during the whole time of
the insurrection, not one of them persuaded the people to desist or showed
them it was high treason. Otherwise he believes in his conscience they
would not have gone forward, for all the people with whom he had
intelligence thought they had not offended the King, as the gentlemen
caused proclamations to be made in his name. He thinks the gentlemen
might have stayed the people of Horncastle, for at the beginning his
parishioners went forward among the rebels only by command of the
gentlemen. The gentlemen were first harnessed of all others, and
commanded the commons to prepare themselves harness, and he believes
the commons expected to have redress of grievances by way of supplication
to the King.

*Letters and Papers of Henry VIII, xii (1), 70 (xi) [68 pp. 21, 24–5].*

DOCUMENT 3 THE YORK ARTICLES, 1536

*These are the articles which Robert Aske wrote out and sent to the mayor of York when he yielded to the Pilgrims' summons on 15 October.*

To the Kyng our Soveraign lorde.

1. The suppression of so many religiouse howses as are at this instant tyme suppressed, whereby the service of our God is not wel [maintained] but also the [commons] of yor realme by unrelieved, the which as we think is a gret hurt to the common welthe and many sisters be [put] from theyr levyings and left at large.

2. The second article is that we humbly beseache your grace that the acte of use may be suppressed because we think by the sayd act we your true subjects be clearly restrayned of yor liberties in the declaration of our wylles concernying our landes, as well for payment of our dettes, for doeing of yor grace service, as for helping and alevying of our children, the which we had by the ... of yor lawes by ... the which as we think is a gret hurt and ... to the commonwelth.

3. The iiide article is that weyr your grace hath a taxe or a quindeyne granted unto you by act of parliament payable the next year, the which is and hath been ever leveable of shepe and catals, and the shepe and catals of yor subjects within the sayde shire are now at this instant tyme in manner utterly decayed and ... whereby your grace to take the sayde tax or quindeyn yor sayde subjects shalbe distrayned to paye iiiid for every beast and xiid for xxtie shepe, the which wold be an importunate charge to them considering the poverty that they be in all redye and losse which they have sutayned these ii years by past.

4. The iiiith article is that we wor yor true subjects thinke that yor grace takes of yor counsell and being a boute you such persons as be of low byrth and small reputation which hath procuryed the proffits most especially for theyr own advantage, the which we suspect to be the lord cromwell and Sir Richard Riche Chanceler of the augmentations.

5. The vth article is that we your true subjects fynd us grevyd that there be diverse bisshopes of England of yor Graces late promosion that hath ... the faith of Christ, as we thinke, which are the bisshops of Canterbury, the bisshop of Rochester, the bisshop of Worcester, the bisshop of Salisbury, the bisshop of Saint Davids, and the bisshop of Dublyn, and in especiall we thynk the begynyngs of all the trouble of that ... and the vexation that hath been ... of yor subjects the bisshop of Lincoln.

*Letters and Papers of Henry VIII, xi, 705 (1).*

DOCUMENT 4  THE OATH OF THE HONOURABLE
MEN, 1536

*Robert Aske later explained that he 'made and devised the Oath ... without
any other man's advice' before the council of the Pilgrim captains held at
York on 17 October. Here it was administered to the gentlemen and it was
then taken by all the Pilgrims.*

Ye shall not enter into this our Pilgrimage of Grace for the Commonwealth,
but only for the love that ye do bear unto Almighty God his faith, and the
Holy Church militant and the maintenance thereof, to the preservation of
the King's person and his issue, to the purifying of the nobility, and to
expulse all villein blood and evil councillors against the commonwealth
from his Grace and his Privy Council of the same. And that ye shall not
enter into our said Pilgrimage for no particular profit to yourself, nor to do
any displeasure to any private person, but by counsel of the commonwealth,
nor slay nor murder for no envy, but in your hearts put away fear and
dread, and take afore you the Cross of Christ, and in your hearts His faith,
the Restitution of the Church, the suppression of these Heretics and their
opinions, by all the holy contents of this book.

*Letters and Papers of Henry VIII, xi, 705 (4) [118 p. 209].*


DOCUMENT 5  ROBERT ASKE TO THE LORDS AT
PONTEFRACT, 1536

*Robert Aske wrote this account of his interview with the lords and gentry at
Pontefract on 19 October when he was in London in December 1536. It
was written at Henry's request.*

And to the lords temporal, the said Aske declared they had misused
themselves, in that they, semblable, had not so providently ordered and
declared to his said highness the poverty of his realm, and that part
specially, and wherein their griefs might ensue, whereby all dangers might
have been avoided; for insomuch as in the north parts much of the relief of
the commons was by succour of abbeys, and that before this last statute
thereof made, the King's highness had no money out of that shire in a
manner yearly, for his grace's revenues there yearly went to the finding of
Berwick. And that now the profits of abbeys suppressed, tenths and first
fruits, went out of those parts. By occasion whereof, within short space or
years, there should be no money nor treasure in those parts, neither the
tenant to have to pay his rents to the lord, nor the lord to have money to
do the King service withal, for so much as in those parts was neither the

presence of his grace, execution of his laws, nor yet but little recourse of merchandise, so that of necessity the said country should either paryssh with the Scots, or of very poverty enforced to make commotion or rebellions; and that the lords knew the same to be true and had not done their duty, for that they had not declared the said poverty of the said country to the King's highness, and the danger that otherwise to his grace would ensue, alleging the whole blame to them the nobility therein with other like reasons.

*Letters and Papers of Henry VIII*, xii (1) 6 [3 *p. 335*; 44 *p. 186*].

DOCUMENT 6    THE PILGRIMS' BALLAD, 1536

The Pilgrims' Ballad is thought to have been composed by the monks of Sawley Abbey in Lancashire. It has sixteen verses in all. This is only one of a number of rhymes circulated during the rising which combined the themes of the Church in danger and the material needs of the commons.

| I | | II | |
|---|---|---|---|
| | Crist crucifyd! | | Gret godes fame |
| | For they woundes wide | | Doith Church proclame |
| | Us commens guyde! | | Now to be lame |
| | Which pilgrames be, | | And fast in boundes, |
| | Thrughe godes grace, | | Robbyd, spoled and shorne |
| | For to purchache | | From catell and corne, |
| | Olde welth and peax | | And clene furth borne |
| | Of the Spiritualtie. | | Of housez and landes. |
| X | | XI | |
| | Alacke! Alacke! | | For ther they hadde |
| | For the church sake | | Boith ale and breyde |
| | Pore comons wake, | | At tyme of nede, |
| | And no marvell! | | And succer grete |
| | For clere it is | | In alle distresse |
| | The decay of this | | And hevyness |
| | How the pore shall mys | | And wel intrete. |
| | No tong can tell. | | |
| XXI | | XVI | |
| | In troubil and care, | | Crim, crame, and riche |
| | Where that we were | | With thre ell and the liche |
| | In maner all bere | | As sum men teache |
| | Of our substance, | | God theym amend! |
| | We found good bate | | And that Aske may, |
| | At churche men gate, | | Without delay, |
| | Without checkmate | | Here make a stay |
| | Or varyaunce. | | And well to end. |

*Letters and Papers of Henry VIII*, xi, 786 (3) [3 *pp. 344–5*].

DOCUMENT 7   THE COMMONS OF WESTMORLAND TO
LORD DARCY, 1536

*This letter of the Pilgrim captains in Westmorland to ask Lord Darcy's
advice is the only evidence of their demands.*

... Consernynge the gyrsums for power men to be a laid a parte but only
penny for penny gyrsum, with all the tythes to remayne to every man hys
owne, doynge therfor accordynge to their dewtye, also taxes casten emongst
the benefest men, as well them in abbett with in us as thai that is not
incumbent for the commenwelthe. Which we dyssyre of your lordship to
tendre up your plesur thairin watt we may do in all these causes for we
thinke in our oppynon thatt we may putt in thair reowmes to serve God
oder that wald be glad to keep hospytallyte for sum of tham are no preestes
that hath the benefyce in hand and oder of tham is my lord Cromwell
chapplaynes ... we accept no gentyllman of our counsel because we be
affrayed of ...

*Letters and Papers of Henry VIII, xi, 1080.*

DOCUMENT 8   ADVICE TO THE PILGRIMS AT
PONTEFRACT

*This anonymous petition of advice to the Pilgrims assembled at Pontefract
has been convincingly attributed to Sir Thomas Tempest, who was ill and
unable to attend in person. He had sat in the parliament of 1529–36 as
member for Newcastle-upon-Tyne. Aske seems to have been influenced by it
at several points in drawing up the final articles.*

My powre advyce to my lorde captayne, baronage and comynaltie at Pomf
[rete] undyr ynsurreccyon that may be resuvyd with sysche of the Kyng's
counsell as cummythe to Duncaster, where by me semys the Kyng schuld
[condescend to] owr petecyon agaynst the Lowler and [trai]tur Thomas
Crumwell, hys dyscypyles and adherentes or at leste exyle hym and theym
furthe of the relm.
    Firste, where yt ys a legyd that we schulde not tayke upon us to assyne
his Gr[ace's Council] yt ys necessary that vertuus men that luffythe the
communwelthe schulde be of his [counci]l ... susche vertuus men as woylde
regarde the communwelthe abuffe their princys ... in this nobyll reym who
reydes the crownakylls of Edwarde the ii what juperdy he was in for Peres
de G[ave]stun, Spenseres, and susche lyke cunsellars and ... Rycharde the ii
was deposyd for folowing the cunsell of susche lyke. Item, a prynce schulde
be mayde Kynge to defende the realme, and rewle hys subietes vertuus[ly]

be iutece myxyd with mercy and pyty, and not undur dysplesur by rygore to [p]u[t] men to de[the], for thowghe yt ys sayde that our bodes [be] the Kynges when he hayse kyllyd a man he [cannot] mayk a man a lyffe ayene.

Item, where yt ys alegyd that the Kynge haythe [au]toryte grantyd hym by parlamente to suppres theys abbays, I thynke that theys parlamentes was of nune actoryte nor vertu, for yff theys schulde be trewly namyd, they shulde be callyd counsylles of the Kynges [a]poyntment, and not parlaments, for parlamentes owyt to have the knyghtes of schyar and bur[gesses for the t]owyns [at] ther owyne electyon that colde resun for the wellthe of the schyar or towyn ... a parlament they have devysyd that men may not speke off the Kynges vycys whysch men may say trewly had moste nede to be spokyn on, and reformyd off [all] thyng, [for if] the hede ayke how can the body be hole ... but what so ever Crumwell says ys ryght and noyne but that.

Item, the false flatterer says he will make the King the richest prince in Christendom, but a man can have no more of us than we have, which in manner he has already, and yet not satisfied. I think he goes about to make him the poorest prince in Christendom, for when by such pillage he has lost the hearts of his baronage and poor commons, the riches of the realm are spent and his oath and faith broken, who will then love or trust him?

... hys servandes and ek hys servandes servandes thynkes to have the law in every playse here oyrderyd at their commandment, and wyll tayk upon thayme to commande scheryffe, justyays of peyse, coram, and of secyon in their mayster's name at their plesure, wytnes Brabsun and Dakynes, so that what so ever thay wyll have doyne must be lawfull, and who contrarys thaym shall be accusyd off tresun, be he never so trew a man.

*Letters and Papers of Henry VIII*, xi, 1244.

DOCUMENT 9    THE PONTEFRACT ARTICLES, 1536

*The document is headed 'Copie of the articles to the Lordes of the King's Counsell at our comyng to Pontefract'. It can therefore be dated to 2–4 December.*

1. The fyrst touchyng our faith to have the heresies of Luther, Wyclif, Husse, Malanton, Ellecumpadus, Bucerus, Confessio Gemaniae, Apologia Malanctionis, the Works of Tyndall, of Barnys, of Marshall, of Rastall, Seynt Germayne and such other heresies of Anibaptist thereby within this realm to be annulled and destroyed.
2. The iid to have the supreme head of the church touching cure animarum to be restored unto the see of Rome as before it was accustomyd to be, and to have the consecracions of the bysshops from hym without any first frutes or pencion to hym to be payd out of this realme or else a pension reasonable for the outward defence of our faith.

3. Item we humbly beseche our most dred sovereign lorde that the Lady Mary may be made legitimate and the former statute therein annulled, for the danger of the title that myght incurre to the crown of Scotland, that to be by parliament.

4. Item to have the abboyes suppressed to be restoryd unto theyr howses land and goodes.

5. Item to have the tenth and fyrst frutes clerely discharged of the same, onles the clergy wyll of themselvys graunte a rent charge in generality to the augmentacion of the crown.

6. Item to have the Freres Observauntes restorid unto ther houses agayn.

7. Item to have the heretiques, bisshoppes and temporall, and their secte to have condigne punyshment by fyer or such other, or ells to trye their quarell with us and our partie takers in batell.

8. Item to have the lord Cromwell, the Lord Chancellor, and Sir Richard Riche kniyght to have condyne punyshment, as the subverters of the good laws of this realm and maynteners of the false sect of those heretiques and the first inventors and bryngands in of them.

9. Item that the landes in Westmorland, Cumberland, Kendall, Dent, Sedber, Fornes and the abbayes landes in Mashamshire, Kyrkbyshire, Notherdale may be by tenant right, and the lord to have at every change ii years rent for gressom and no more according to the grante now made by the lordes to the commons there under ther seall. And this to be done by act of parliament.

10. Item the statutes of handgunnys and crossbowes to be repelled, and the ... thereof onles it be in the Kings Forest or parkes for the kylling of his graces deer red and fallow.

11. Item that doctor Ligh and doctor Layton ... have condigne punyshment for theyr extortions in theyr tyme of visitactions, as in [taking?] from religiouse howses xl li, xx li, and so to ... summys, horses, ... leases, under ... brybes by them taken, and of theyr abhominable actes by them comytted and done.

12. Item reformation for the election of knights of shire and burgesses, and for the uses amonge the lordes in the parliament howse after theyr auncient custome.

13. Item statute for inclosors and intacks to be put in execution, and that all intaks inclosors sith Anno iiii h. vii to be pulled down except mountains, forest and parkes.

14. Item to be discharged of the quindene and taxes now granted by acte of parliament.

15. Item to have the parliament in a convenient place at Nottyngham or York and the same shortly somonyd.

16. Item the statute of the declaracion of the crown by wyll, that the same may be annulled and repellyd.

17. Item that it be inactid by acte of parliamente that all recognisances, statutes, penalties new forfayt during the tyme of this comocion may be pardonyd and discharged as well agaynst the King as strangers.

18. Item the privlages and rights of the church to be confirmed by acte of parliament, and prestes not suffre by sourde onless he be disgrecid, a man to be savid by his book, sanctuary to save a man for all causes in extreme nede, and the church for xl daies and further according to the laws as they were used in the begynnyng of this kings days.

19. Item the liberties of the church to have ther old custemys as the county palatyn at Durham, Beverlay, Ruppon, Sanct Peter of York and such other by act of parliament.

20. Item to have the statute that no man shall wyll hys lands to be repellid.

21. Item that the statutes of tresons for wordes and such tyke made since Anno xxi of our sovereign lord that now is to be in like wyse repelled.

22. Item that the common lawes mai have place as was used in the begynning of your graces reyne and that all iniunctions may be clerely vewyed and not to be granted onles the mater be hard and determyned in the chancery.

23. Item that no man upon subpoena is from Trent north to apeyr but at York or by attornay onles it be directid uppon payn of allegeance and for lyke maters concernyng the kyng.

24. Item a remedy ageynst escheators for fyndyng of fals offices and extorsious fees, taking which be not holdyn of the kyng and ageynst the ... thereof.

*Letters and Papers of Henry VIII*, xi, 1246.

DOCUMENT 10     **RICHARD MORISON:** *A REMEDY FOR SEDITION*, **1536**

*In 1536 Richard Morison returned to England after living in the household of Reginald Pole at Padua. His passage home was paid by Thomas Cromwell and he at once became one of the leading Cromwellian publicists [46, Ch. 4; 142]. His book A Remedy for sedition was printed by Berthelet, the king's printer, within a few weeks of the outbreak of the Pilgrimage of Grace.*

When every man wyll rule, who shalt obeye? Nowe can there be any commune welthe, where he that is welthiest, is mooste lyke to come to woo? Who can there be ryche, where he that is rychest is in mooste daunger of povertie? No, no, take welthe by the hande, and say farewell welth, where lust is lyked, and lawe refused, where uppe is sette downe, and downe sette uppe: An order, and order muste be hadde, and a waye founde that they rule that beste can, they be ruled, that mooste it becommeth so to be. This agreement is not onely expedient, but also most necessary in a commonwelthe, those that are of the worser sort, to be content, that they wyser rule and governe theym, those that nature hath endued with syngular vertues, and fortune without breache of lawe, sette in high dignitie, to suppose this done by the great provydence of god, as a meane to engender love and amitie, betwene the high and the lowe, the smalle and the great, the one beinge so necessarye for the others savegarde welthe and quietnes. For as there must be some men of polycie and prudence, to discerne what is metest to be done in the government of states even so there must be other of strength and redynes, to do what the wyser shall thinke expedient, bothe for the mayntenance of them that governe, and for the schuyng of the infinite jeoperdies, that a multitude not governed fallith into: These must not go, arme in arme, but the one before, the other behynde ...

A comune welthe is lyke a body, and soo lyke, that it can be resembled to nothyng so convenient, as unto that. Nowe, were it not by your faythe, a madde herynge, if the fote shuld say, I wyl weare a cappe with an ouche, as the heade dothe? If the knees shulde say, we woll carie the eyes, an other wyle: if the shulders shulde clayme eche of them an eare: if the heles wold nowe go before, and the toes behind? This were undoubted a mad heryng: every man wold say, the fete, the knees, the shoulders the heles make unlaufull requestes, and very madde petitions. But if it were so in dede, if the fote had a cap, the knees eies, the shulders eares, what a monstrous body shulde this be? God sende them suche a one, that shal at any time go about to make as evil a comune welth, as this is a body. It is not mete, every man to do, that he thinketh best.

DOCUMENT 11    **THE EXAMINATION OF
ROBERT ASKE, 1537**

*Aske was examined about every aspect of his part in the Pilgrimage during his imprisonment in the Tower in April and May 1537. Both the interrogatories and his replies have been preserved.*

To the statut of subpressions, he dyd gruge ayenst the same and so did al the holl contrey, because the abbeys in the north partes gaf great almons to pour men and laudable servyd God; in which partes of lait dais they had but smal comfort by gostly teching. And by occasion of the said suppression the devyn service of almightie God is much minished, greate nombre of messes unsaid, and the blissed consecracion of the sacrament now not used and showed in thos places, to the distreas of the faith, and sperituall comfort to man soull, the temple of God russed and pulled down, the ornamentes and releques of the church of God unreverent used, the townes and sepulcres of honourable and noble men pulled down and sold, non hospitalite now in thos places kept, but the fermers for the most parte lettes and taverns out the fermes of the same houses to other fermers, for lucre and advauntage to them selfes. And the profites of thies abbeys yerley goith out of the contrey to the Kinges highnes, so that in short space little money, by occasion of the said yerly rentes, tenementes and furst frutes, should be left in the said countrey, in consideracion of the absens of the Kinges highnes in thos partes, want of his lawes and the frequentacion of merchandisse. Also diverse and many of the said abbeys wer in the montaignes and desert places, wher the people be rud of condyccions and not well taught the law of God and when the said abbeys stud, the said peuple not only had worldly refreshing in their bodies but also sperituall refuge both by gostly liffing of them and also by spiritual informacion, and preching; and many ther tenauntes wer ther feed servaundes to them, and serving men, wel socored by abbeys; and now not only theis tenauntes and servauntes wantes refresshing ther, both of meat, cloth and wages, and knowith not now wher to have any liffing, but also strangers and baggers of corne as betwix Yorkshir, Lancashir, Kendall, Westmoreland and the bishopreke, was nither cariage of come and merchandise, greatly socored both horsse and man by the said abbeys, for non was in thes partes denyed, nether horsemeat nor manesmeat so that the people was greatlie refresshyed by the said abbeys, wher now they have no such succour; and wherfor the said statut of subpression was greatly to the decay of the comyn welth of that contrei and al thos partes of al degreys greatly groged ayenst the same, and yet doth ther dewtie of allegieance alwais savyd.

Also the abbeys was on of the bewties of this realme to al men and strangers passing threw the same; also al gentilmen much socored in their nedes with money, their yong sons ther socored, and in nonries ther doughters brought up in vertue; and also ther evidenses and mony left to the usses of infantes in abbeys handes, always sure ther; and such abbeys as wer ner the danger of see bankes, great mayntenours of see wals and dykes, maynteours and bilders of briges and heghwais, and such other thinges for the comyn welth.

*Letters and Papers of Henry VIII*, xii (1) 852, 900, 901, 945, 946, 1175. Nos 900, 901 and 945 are printed in full in [3] pp. 550–73.

DOCUMENT 12    THE DEMANDS OF THE WESTERN
             REBELS, 1549

*There are a number of different versions of the rebel articles. That printed here, from* A Copy of a Letter *[Doc. 13], is the most complete and represents the final manifesto drawn up outside Exeter.*

The Articles of us the Commoners of Devonshire and Cornwall in divers Campes by East and West of Excettor.
1. Fyrst we wyll have the general counsall and holy decrees of our forefathers observed, kept and performed, and who so ever shal agayne saye them, we hold them as Heretikes.

2. Item we will have the Lawes of our Soverayne Lord Kyng Henry the viii concernynge the syxe articles, to be in use again, as in hys time they were.

3. Item we will have the masse in Latten, as was before, and celebrated by the Pryest wythoute any man or woman communycatyng wyth hym.

4. Item we wyll have the Sacrement hange over the hyeghe aulter, and there to be worshypped as it was wount to be, and they whiche will not therto consent, we wyl have them dye lyke heretykes against the holy Catholyque fayth.

5. Item we wyll have the Sacrement of the aulter but at Easter delyvered to the lay people, and then but in one kynde.

6. Item we will that our Curattes shal minister the Sacrament of Baptisme at all tymes aswel in the weke daye as on the holy daye.

7. Item we wyl have holy bread and holy water made every sondaye, Palmes and asshes at the tymes accustomed, Images to be set up again in every church, and all other auncient olde Ceremonyes used heretofore, by our mother the holy Church.

8. Item we wil not receyve the newe servyce because it is but lyke a Christmas game, but we wyll have oure olde service of Mattens, masse, Evensong and procession in Latten not in English, masse, Evensong and procession in Latten not in English, as it was before. And so we the Cornyshe men (whereof certen of us understande no Englysh) utterly refuse thys newe Englysh.

9. Item we wyll have everye preacher in his sermon, and every Pryest at hys masse, praye specially by name for the soules in purgatory, as oure forefathers dyd.

10. Item we wyll have the whole Byble and al bokes of scripture in Englysh to be called in agayn, for we be enformed that otherwise the Clergye, shal not of long time confound the heretykes.

11. Item we wyll have Doctor Moreman and Doctor Crispin which holde our opinions to be savely sent unto us and to them we requyre the Kinges maiesty, to geve some certain lyvinges, to preach amonges us our Catholycke fayth.

12. Item we thinke it very mete because the lord Cardinal Pole is of the kynges bloode, should not only have hys free pardon, but also sent for to Rome and promoted to be first or second of the kinges counsayl.

13. Item we wyll that no Gentylman shall have anye mo servantes then one to wayte upon hym excepte he maye dispende one hundreth marke land and for every hundreth marke we thynke it reasonable, he should have a man and no mo.

14. Item we wyll that the halfe parte of the abbey landes and Chauntrye landes, in everye mans possessyons, how so ever he cam by them, be geven again to two places, where two of the chief Abbeis was with in every Countye, where suche half part shalbe taken out, and there to be establyshed a place for devout persons, whych shall pray for the Kyng and the common wealth, and to the same we wyll have al the almes of the Churche box geven for these seven yeres, and for thys article we desire that we may name half of the Commissioners.

15. Item for the particular grieffes of our Countrye, we wyll have them so ordered, as Hunfreye Arundell, and Henry Braye the Kynges Maior of Bodman, shall enforme the Kynges Maiestye, yf they maye have salve-conduct under the Kynges great Seale, to passe and repasse, with an Heroalde of Armes.

16. Item for the performance of these articles we will have iiii Lordes viii Knightes xii Esquyers xx Yomen, pledges with us until the Kynges Maiestie have graunted al these by Parliament.

The articles are signed by the five 'chiefe captaynes' and 'the foure Governours of the Campes'.

Transcript from the Lambeth Palace Library copy with the addition of the sixteenth article from the copy in Corpus Christi College, Oxford [109 *App. K and pp. 222–3*].

DOCUMENT 13    *A COPY OF A LETTER*, 1549

*Extract from* A Copy of a Letter, printed tract of 1549. The letter was written by a gentleman of Devon on 27 July and gives a first-hand account of the rebellion and an analysis of its causes. There is some evidence to suggest that the recipient at Court, Mr C., can be identified as Secretary Cecil. The letter comments on the price rise, the attitudes of gentry to their livings and the rebels' article on abbey and chantry lands.

And if the comon people shalbe eased of their griefes, the gentlemen shall be relieved of them, for se how much the fermour crieth out of the market, the one as muche greved as the other, and one remedye I trust shal serve both. For me thinketh it is no more difference for me, to have xx pound, spendyng xx pound, than to have xx marke spendinge xx marke so that my estate be kept like with both, you wyll thynke I wryte now at my wyl, because yf ye remember the last yere in the parke at Wynsour when the Court was there, thys question made great argument betwyxte you and me, whether for the amendment of thinges in the common wealthe the fermour should fyrst abate hys pryce, and then the Landed man his rent, or in contrary order, at whyche tyme, I remembre you stode upon one poynte, which I could not denye, that the Gentylman by deere byeng, was dryven to let deere, and I upon the other poynte (not al untrewe) that the deere hyrynge made a deere sellynge. But where the fault fyrst beganne, neyther of us woulde graunt to the other, neverthelesse, so wayghty a matter it is, as so no wayes to be discussed but by Parliament. Where when the argument is at an ende, it may be establyshed by a lawe, wherof there was never more lykelyhood, because the amendment thereof, wyl helpe so many as well Lordes and Gentilmen, as al other Commoners, no man havyng cause to repyne agaynst it, but suche as gather, not to spende and improve their lyvinges not for their charges, as many Gentilmen have done, but for their coffers. So that to conclude improvement alone maketh no man ryche, but improvement and sparynge. But what medle I wyth thys matter, and yet what dare I not to you my fryende, by Sayncte George I saye to you merely out of bourde, no one thinge maketh me more angry with these rebelles than one article, which toucheth me on the quicke, and I believe, there be few in the realme but it will make them smart, to forgoe his Abbey and Chauntrye landes wherein I for my part am so heated, that if I should fight wyth those traitours, I wold for every two strokes to be stricken for treason strike on to kepe my lands, the which I bought to suerlye, to deliver it at a papistes appoyntement.

Transcript from the Lambeth Palace Library copy [109 *App. K*].

DOCUMENT 14    **PHILIP NICHOLS'S ANSWER TO THE COMMONERS OF DEVONSHIRE AND CORNWALL, 1549**

*This tract, which had long been attributed to Nicholas Udall, has now been convincingly shown to have been written by the Devon Protestant, Philip Nichols, a skilled controversialist who was at that time also involved in debate with the Canon of Exeter, Richard Crispin [140 p. 115].*

What other fruit or end may hereof ensue unto you but devouring one another and an universal desolation of your own selves, besides the extreme peril of God's high wrath and indignation, besides the undoubted plague of mortality which (unless ye call for mercy in season) must needs light upon you by the severe rod of princely justice in our realm. Ye do in the meantime neglect your husbandry, whereby ye must live: your substance and catall is not only spoiled and spent upon unthriftes, who but for this your outrage know no mean nor way to be fedde: your houses falle in ruin, your wives are ravished, your daughters defloured before your own faces, your goods that ye have many long years laboured for lost in an hour and spent upon vagabonds and idle loiterers. Your meat is unpleasant, your drink unsavoury, your sleep never sound, never quiet, never in any safety. What must befal to your children hereafter when your own living is thus through your own folly brought to penury and famine ...

What shall be said of you an hundred years hereafter when cronycles shall report that a certain portion of the English people called Devonsheir men and Cornishmen did for popery (which if God be God will long ere that day be utterly confounded and defaced and the name thereof throughout all the Christen world abhorred and detested) did rebel against their natural sovereign lord and king, most earnestly travailing to set forth and publish the true word of God and the true religion of Christ unto them.

B.L. Royal MS, 18 B. xi fol. 1; N. Pocock, 'Troubles connected with the Prayer Book of 1549', Camden Society, new series, vol. xxxvii, 1884, p. 145.

DOCUMENT 15    THE COUNCIL TO THE JUSTICES OF THE PEACE OF DEVON, 1549

*This letter and the one following show how the government's attitude to the Western Rebellion changed as its seriousness became apparent.*

... We require you to traveyll by fayr meannes eyther openly with the hole world, or els apart with the ringleaders by all the best ways you can devise to induce them to retyre to ther houses, putting them and especially the cheff doers among them in rememberance what an onnaturall dealing this is of subjects to rise against ther soveraigne lord. What onkindness his Majesty may herafter justly conceyve herof sens these things be attempted in his mynorite. Whatt dyshonor and onsuertie to the hole realme may grow by these attemptats. Whatt courage the hearing therof shall administer to the Frenchmen, Scots our enemyes, to putt them in remembraunce that the parts of good and obedient subjects hadd byn ffyrst to have sued for remedie att the hands of ther soveraign lord, and nott to take upon themselfs the swerd and authorite to redresse as they list, especially those maters which being allredye established by a law and consent of the hole realme can nott (if anything was to be reformed) bee otherwise altered then by a law agayn. By these or such other good words you may fyrst assay to asswage then wherein if you shall not be hable to satisfie them, yett shall you by these meannes somewhat mitigate their furor, and use the meannes you possably can best devyse to stay the comyng of gretter nombers unto them, and in the mean tyme putt your selfs with such of your tenaunts and servants as you best trust, secretly ordered to attend such further direction as our very good lord, the lord pryvey seall, who is now in journey towards you, shall farthar prescribe. As for the delay of a tyme for th'execution of the statute of the shepe and cloth we have written more amply to you by our former letters, and thus eftsones requiring you to joyn wysely and manly together in these things, we bydd you hartily farewell.

From Syon. To Sir Thomas Denys, Peter Courteney and Antony Harvy, Justices of the Peace in Devon, xxvith of June 1549.

Public Record Office, S.P. 10/7/42 (*Calendar of State Papers Domestic, Edward VI*, no. 287); N. Pocock, 'Troubles connected with the Prayer Book of 1549', Camden Society, new series, vol. xxxvii, 1884, p. 12.

DOCUMENT 16    THE COUNCIL TO LORD RUSSELL, 1549

Frome my L. protector and the Consell to my L. Pryvie Seall, lieutenant to the Kynge's Majestie in the west parties.

... Where ye declare that thoccasyon of being able to levie so fewe in Somersetshire is the evil inclynation of the people, and that there are amongs them that do not styck openly to speak such traterous words agaynst the kyng and in favour of the trayterous rebells. Ye shall hang two or three of them, and cause them to be executed lyke traytors. And that wilbe the only and the best staye of all those talks.

As to them that maketh dyverse excuses and will not serve the kyngs Majestie, ye shall cause them to be noted especially the chiefe doers, and in your retorne they may be ordered according to theyr deserts. Though ye think proclamations can do no great good, so as we wrote unto you made, yet they may do you some good. Hurt they can do none. ... We do lyke well yor ordering of the ringleaders, and recon no lesse then you do that sharpe justice must be executed upon those sondrie traytors which will learne by nothing but by the sword.

Frome Westminster the xxviith of Julii.

Inner Temple Petyt MS, 538, vol. 46, fol. 444; N. Pocock, 'Troubles connected with the Prayer Book of 1549', Camden Society, new series, vol. xxxvii, 1884, p. 40.

DOCUMENT 17    'KETT'S DEMANDS BEING IN
                REBELLION', 1549

*The only surviving copy of the articles headed as above has attached to it the names of the representatives of twenty-two hundreds in Norfolk, together with those of Suffolk and the city of Norwich.*

1. We pray your grace that where it is enacted for inclosyng that it be not hurtfull to suche as have enclosed saffren grounds for they be gretly chargeablye to them, and that from hensforth noman shall enclose any more.
2. We certifie your grace that where as the lords of the manours hath byn charged with certen fre rent, the same lords hath sought meanes to charge the freholders to pay the same rent, contrarye to right.
3. We pray your grace that no lord of no mannor shall comon upon the Comons.
4. We pray that prests frome hensforth shall purchase no londs neyther ffre nor Bondy, and the lands that they have in possession may be letten to temporall men, as they wer in the fyrst yere of the reign of Kyng henry the vii.

5. We pray that Redeground and medowe grounde may be at suche price as they wer in the first yere of Kyng henry the vii.

6. We pray that all marshysshe that ar holden of the Kyngs majestie by ffre rent or of any other, may be ageyn at the price that they wer in the ffirst yere of King henry the vii.

7. We pray that all Bushells within your realme be of one stice, that is to sey, to be in mesure viii gallons.

8. We pray that prests or vicars that be not able to preche and sett forth the woorde of god to hys parisheners may be thereby putt from hys benyfice, and the parisheners there to chose an other or else the pateron or lord of the towne.

9. We pray that the payments of castillward rent, and blanche fferme,and office lands, which hath been accostomed to be gathered of the tenaments, where as we suppose the lords ought to pay the same to ther balyffs for the rents gatheryng, and not the tenants.

10. We pray that noman under the degre of a knyght or esquyer kepe a dowe howse, except it hath byn of an ould anchyent costome.

11. We pray that all ffreholders and copieholders may take the profights of all comons, and ther to comon, and the lords not to comon nor take profights of the same.

12. We pray that no Feodorye within your shires shalbe a counceller to eny man in his office makyng, wherby the Kyng may be trulye served, so that a man beeng of good consyence may be verely chosyn to the same office by the comons of the same sheyre.

13. We pray your grace to take all libertie of lete into your owne hands whereby all men may quyetly enjoye ther comons with all profights.

14. We pray that copiehould land that is onresonable rented may go as it dyd in the first yere of Kyng henry vii and that at the deth of a tenante or of a sale the same lands to be charged with an esey ffyne as a capon or a reasonable some of money for a remembraunce.

15. [We pray that no] prest [shall be a chaplain] nor no other officer to eny man of honor or wyrshypp but ony to be resydent uppon ther benefices whereby ther parysheners may be enstructed with the lawes of god.

16. We pray thatt all bonde men may be made ffre for god made all ffre with his precious blode sheddyng.

17. We pray that Ryvers may be ffre and comon to all men for fyshyng and passage.

18. We pray that noman shallbe put by your Eschetory and Feodrie to ffynde eny office unless he holdeth of your grace in cheyff or capite above £10 a year.

19. We pray that the pore mariners or Fysherman may have the hole profights of ther fyshyngs as purpres grampes whalles or any grett fyshe so it be not prejudiciall to your grace.

20. We pray that evry propriatorie parson or vicar havyng a benefice of £10 or more by yere shall eyther by themselves or by some other persone teche pore mens chyldren of ther paryshe the boke called the cathakysme and the prymer.

21. We pray that it be not lawfull to the lords of eny mannor to purchase londs frely and to lett then out ageyn by copie of court roll to ther gret advaunchement and to the undoyng of your pore subjects.

22. We pray that no proporiatorie parson or vicar in consideracon of advoyding trobyll and sute betwyn them and ther pore parishners whiche they daly do procede and attempt shall from hensforth take for the full contentacon of all the tenthes which nowe they do receyve but viiid. of the noble in the full discharge of all other tythes.

23. [We pray that no man under] the degre of [esquyre] and shall kepe any conyes upon any of ther owne frehold or copiehold onles he pale them in so that it shall not be to the comons noysoyns.

24. We pray that no person of what estate degre or condicion he be shall from hensforth sell the adwardshyppe of eny chyld but that the same chyld if he lyve to his full age shall be at his owne chosyn concernyng his marriage the Kyngs wards only except.

25. We pray that no manner of person havyng a mannor of his owne shall be no other lords balyf but only his owne.

26. We pray that no lord knyght nor gentleman shall have or take in ferme any spirituall promocion.

27. We pray your grace to gyve lycens and aucthorite by your gracious comyssion under your grett seall to suche comyssioners as your pore comons hath chosyn, or to as many of them as your majestie and your consell shall apoynt and thynke mete, for to redresse and reforme all suche good lawes, statutes, proclamacions, and all other your procedyngs, whiche hath byn hydden by your Justices of your peace, Shreves, Escheatores, and others your officers, from your pore comons, synes the first yere of the reigne of your noble grandfather King henry the seventh.

28. We pray that those your officers that hath offended your grace and your comons and so provid by the compleynt of your pore comons do gyve onto these pore men so assembled iiiid every day so long as they have remayned ther.

29. We pray that no lorde knyght esquyer nor gentleman do graze nor fede eny bullocks or shepe if he may spende forty pounds a yere by his lands but only for the provicion of his howse.

By me Robt Kett   Thomas Cod
By me Thomas Aldryche

B.L. Harleian MS, 304, fol. 75 [112 *p. 48*].

DOCUMENT 18   **NICHOLAS SOTHERTON: THE COMMOYSON IN NORFOLK, 1549**

*Nicholas Sotherton's account was written from the viewpoint of the gentry. It emphasizes the element of class conflict in the rebellion.*

They appoynted a place of ascemblye emonge them in an oken tre in that place, which they bordid to stand on. Uppon which two at ye first did none come but Kett and the rest of the Gouvernours where the people oute of wer admonishid to be ware of their robbinge spoylinge and other theyr evil demeanors and what accompte they had to make. But that lyttil prevailid for they cryid out of the Gentlemen as well for that they would not pull downe theyr enclosid growndis, as allsoe understood they by letters fownd emonge theyr sarvants how they sowt by all weyes to suppres them, and whatsoever was sayde they would downe with them soe that within a ii or iii wekes they had so pursuyd the Gentlemen from all parts that in noe place durst one Gentleman keepe his house but were faine to spoile themselves of theyr apparrell and lye and keepe in woods and lownde placis where no resorte was: and some fledd owte of the countrye and gladd they were in theyr howses for saving of the rest of theyr goods and cattell to provide for them daiely bred mete drinke and all other viands and to carry the same at their charge even home to the rebellis campe, and that for the savinge theyr wyves, and chydren and sarvants.

All other municion they gatt by force owt of the cytie and commanded every cytezin to bee to them assistant, setting their face to bee the kings ffreinds and to defend the Kings Laws soe impudent were they now become: yea now they would noe more been advertizid by their Governours but theyr Governors must concent to them and by this farr had they not only all Gentyllmen and yeomen att theyr commandment but for the most of Estimacion in the cyttie whereuppon dyvers of the best cytezins with theyr wyves, children, were faine to depart the cittye for that they would by noe meanis obey them and spare up their occupyeng and otheyr theyr substance in secret wyse which understandid, from thence furth were accompid of the rebellis as Traytors and they in the Campe made Havock of all they could gett ... when the state of the cyttie began to bee in most mysserable case, that all men looked for utter destruction both of lyfe and goods ... and the Gentyllmen they tooke they browte to the tree of Reformacion to bee seene of the people to demande what they would doe with them: when some cryide hang him and some kill him and some that heard noe word cryd even as the rest even when themselvis being demandid why they cryd answerd for that theyr fellows afore did the like, and indeede they did presse theyr weapons to kyll some of those Gentyllmen browte to them which they did of such malice that one Mr Wharton being garded with a Lane of men on both sydes from the said tre into the cyttie they pricked him with theyr spears and other weapons on purpose to kill him had they not had greate helpe to withstand theer malice and creweltye, and further the rest of the Gentyllmenne imprisoned they fettrid with chenis and Locks and pointid divers to ward them for escapinge and in the mean tyme with Kett's authority both Constables and other officers enforcid with theyr company to keepe the Gates that the cytezins shuld not soe fast range furth the cyttie as allsoe that noe Gentyllmenne shuld escape.

B.L. Harleian MS, 1576, fols 252–3 [7 *pp. 83–5*].

DOCUMENT 19    **WILLIAM PAGET TO PROTECTOR SOMERSET, 1549**

*William Paget was one of Somerset's closest advisers. This letter, written on 7 July 1549, is one of a series in which Paget warned the Protector of the dangers of his policy.*

I told your Grace the trouthe, and was not believed: well, now your Grace seithe yt what seythe your Grace? Mary, the King's subjects owt of all discipline, owt of obedience, caryng neither for Protectour nor King, and much lesse for any other meane officer. And what is the cause? Your own levytie, your softnes, your opinion to be good to the pore. I knowe, I saye, your good meaning and honest nature. But I saye, Syr, yt is great pitie (as the common proverbe goeth in a warme summer) that ever fayre wether should do harme. Yt is pitie that your so muche gentlenes should be an occasion of so great an evell as ys now chaunced in England by these rebelles.

Consider, I beseeche youe most humbly, with all my harte, that societie in a realme dothe consiste and ys maynteyned by meane of religion and lawe ... Loke well whether youe have either lawe or religion at home, and I feare youe shall fynde neither. The use of the old religion is forbydden by a lawe, and the use of the newe ys not yet prynted in the stomaches of the eleven of twelve partes in the realme, what countenance soever men make outwardly to please them in whom they see the power restethe. Now, Syr, for the lawe: where ys it used in England at libertie? Almost no where. The fote taketh upon him the parte of the head, and comyns ys become a kinge, appointing condicions and lawes to the governours, sayeng, 'Grant this, and that, and we will go home' ... I knowe in this matter of the commons every man of the Counsayle hath myslyked your procedings, and wyshed it otherways.

Public Record Office, S.P. 10/8/4 (*Calendar of State Papers Domestic, Edward VI*, no. 301).

DOCUMENT 20    **SIR THOMAS WYATT'S SCHEME FOR A LOCAL MILITIA, 1549**

*Wyatt's scheme for a militia to protect the government, following the rebellions of 1549, was described by his son George.*

... my father, and divers of good sort (for it concerned the nobillitie and Gentlemen many waise) concideringe here upon conceavid that the most suer and proper remedie for this headstronge mischife would be to strengthen the Kings part with a power of the choise of his most able and trusty subjects, which might upon a very short warninge in a reddiness, wel armed and ordered against all suddin attemptes, either at home or abrode, and whereby he might not doubt to use without danger his other subjects armed and trained ... against any mightie prince that should make invation upon this realme ...

This thinge thus in general was movid and propounded to the Lord Protectors grace then beinge and to divers others of their Honours of the privie Counsel then unto the King and was withe greate likinge aproved and alowed of but not concluded upon, either for the newnes of the thinge, or for that it was not at that season thought so convenient to have the subiectes armed, whereof the greater numbers were evel affected to the religion then professed, or for that some divition then beinge amongst thos that bare the sway, some hindered that that others liked of. Whereupon, my Father, not withstandinge partly for his private exersise partly that he might have sumthinge reddy for this purpose when a better opertunitie might serve the first waye not taking place, conceived that he with sum of his familiers and companions at many martial bankets, men that had seene and experiensed muche in their travels and servisese abrode and at home, might doe sumwhat that should not be unworthy their travel. ... Thes for the better accomplishinge of this millitary exercise did distribute amongst themselves the sundry parts of this business to those that were best acquainted with the same. Which after was by the rest perused and perfected by one common consent and opinion in such sort as it grew to a large volume ...

B.L. Wyatt MS, 17 [80 *p. 49*; 81 *pp. 55–8*].


## DOCUMENT 21   THE TOWER CHRONICLE, 1554

*'The Chronicle of Queen Jane, and of two years of Queen Mary' is a pocket diary written by an officer in the royal service, resident in the Tower of London at the time of Wyatt's Rebellion.*

The said Wyat, with his men, marched still forwarde all along to Temple barre, also thoroghe Fleete Street, along tyll he cam to Ludgate, his men going not in eny goode order or array. It is saide that in Fleet street certayn of the lorde treasurer's band, to the nomber of ccc men, mett theym, and so going on the one syde passyd by theym coming on the other syde without eny whit saying to them. Also this is more strandge: the saide Wyat and his company passyd along by a great company of harnessyd men, which stoode on both sydes, without eny withstandinge them, and as he marched forwarde through Fleet street, moste with theire swords drawne, some cryed 'Queen Mary hath graunted our request, and geven us pardon'. Others said,

'The quene hath pardoned us'. Then Wyat cam even to Ludgate, and knockyd calling to come in, saying, there was Wyat, whome the quene had graunted their requestes; but the lorde William Howard standing at the gate, saide, 'Avaunt, traytour! thou shalt not come in here'. And then Wyat awhill stayed, and, as some say, rested him apon a seate [at] the Bellsavage gate; at last, seeing he coulde not come in, and belike being deceaved of the ayde which he hoped out of the cetye, retourned backe agayne in arraye towards Charing crosse, and was never stopped tyll he cam to Temple barre, wher certayn horsemen which cam from the felde met them in the face; and then beganne the fight agayne to waxe hot ...

B.L. Harleian MS, 194; Camden Society, first series, vol. xlviii, 1850, pp. 49–50.

DOCUMENT 22   THE PROCLAMATION OF THE EARLS, 1569

*In this proclamation, issued at Darlington on 16 November, the earls used the cause of Catholicism to rally the north. Similar proclamations were issued at Staindrop and Richmond. They all emphasized the earls' determination to restore the 'ancyent customes and usages' in religion.*

Thomas, Earl of Northumberland and Charles, Earl of Westmoreland, the Queens most trewe and lawful subjects, and to all her highness people, sendeth greeting:– Whereas diverse newe set upp nobles about the Quenes Majestie, have and do dailie, not onlie go about to overthrow and put down the ancient nobilitie of this realme, but also have misused the Queens Majesties owne personne, and also have by the space of twelve years nowe past, set upp, and mayntayned a new found religion and heresie, contrarie to Gods word. For the amending and redressing whereof, divers foren powers doo purpose shortlie to invade thes realmes, which will be to our utter destruction, if we do not ourselves speedilie forfend the same. Wherefore we are now constreyned at this tyme to go aboute to amend and redresse it ourselves, which if we shold not do and forenners enter upon us we shold be all made slaves and bondsmen to them. These are therefore to will and require you, and every of you, being above the age of sixteen years and not sixty, as your dutie towards God doth bynde you, for the settinge forthe of his trewe and catholicke religion; and as you tender the common wealth of your countrie, to come and ressort unto us with all spede, with all such armour and furnyture as you, or any of you have. This fail you not herein, as you will answer the contrary at your perills. God save the Quene.

B.L. Harleian MS, 6990, fol. 44; C. Sharp, *Memorials of the Rebellion of 1569*, London, 1840, pp. 42–3.

DOCUMENT 23     SIR RALPH SADLER TO SIR WILLIAM
CECIL, 1569

*In this passage of a report to Cecil from York on 6 December, Sadler*
*explained why Sussex could not trust his forces in open conflict with the*
*rebels.*

I perceive Her Majesty is to believe that the force of her subjects of this
country should not increase, and be able to match with the rebels; but it is
easy to find the cause. There are not ten gentlemen in all this country that
favour her proceedings in the cause of religion. The common people are
ignorant, superstitious, and altogether blinded with the old popish doctrine,
and therefore so favour the cause which the rebels make the colour of their
rebellion, that, though their persons be here with us, their hearts are with
them. And no doubt all this country had wholly rebelled if, at the
beginning, my Lord Lieutenant had not wisely and stoutly handled the
matter. If we should go to the field with this northern force only, they
would fight faintly; for if the father be on this side, the son is on the other;
and one brother with us and the other with the rebels.

*Calendar of State Papers Domestic, Addenda, 1566–79,* vol. xv, 77.

DOCUMENT 24     THE EXAMINATION OF THE EARL OF
NORTHUMBERLAND, 1572

*This is the Earl of Northumberland's own account of the purposes and*
*planning of the rebellion, given in answer to a series of questions put to him*
*by Lord Hunsdon in 1572, when he had been handed over by the Scots. It*
*reveals his hesitancy in entering the conspiracy and shows the extent to*
*which he acted at the instigation of others. The first section transcribed here*
*is Northumberland's account of what happened after the conspirators had*
*received Norfolk's message not to stir.*

Then old Norton and Markenfeld came to me and said we were already in
peril, through our often meetings, and must either enter the matter without
the Earl, or depart the realm; and it would be a great discredit to leave off a
godly enterprise that was looked for at our hands by the whole kingdom,
many of whom would assist us. I bade them take time to consider; they
were away 14 days, and then returned with other gentlemen of the
bishopric, and some belonging to the Earl, who were forward in the matter.
I objected that my Lord President suspected us, and would not let us escape;
but I offered to write to the gentlemen of the country to know their mind.
They answered coldly and that stopped us awhile. I wished to consult the

Earl of Derby, Queen of Scots and Spanish ambassador. The first did not answer; the other two thought it better not to stir.

Then our company was discouraged. I left my house on a false alarm, and went to Lord Westmoreland's on my way to Alnwick. I found with him all the Nortons, Markenfeld, his two uncles, the two Tempests, John Swinburne, and Sir John Nevill, all ready to enter forthwith. We consulted; my Lord, his uncles, old Norton, and Markenfeld were earnest to proceed. Fras. Norton, John Swinburne, myself, and others thought it impossible, so we broke up and departed, every man to provide for himself. Lady Westmoreland, hearing this, cried out, weeping bitterly, that we and our country were shamed for ever, and that we must seek holes to creep into. Some departed, and I wished to go ... but when I found I could not get away, I agreed to rise with them.

When did you first enter into this conspiracy? Ans., We first began to talk of these matters when the Duke went in displeasure from Court to his house in London, and it was bruited in Yorkshire that the Council was wonderfully divided about the succession, that the Duke and other noblemen had retired to their houses, and that the realm would be in a hurly-burly; so I sent to the Duke and assembled my friends, to know their inclinations. I and many gentlemen intended to join the Duke, if the quarrel were for reformation of religion or naming a successor, but not to hazard myself for the marriage. This I fear made my enemies about Her Majesty pick a quarrel with me. On the Duke's repair to court, hearing that the reports about naming a successor were untrue, I sought to forbear to stir ...

What was the intent and meaning of the rebellion? Ans., Our first object in assembling was the reformation of religion and preservation of the person of the Queen of Scots, as next heir, failing issue of Her Majesty, which causes I believed were greatly favoured by most of the noblemen of the realm. I hoped my Lord Leicester, and especially Lord Burghley, with his singular judgment, had by this time been blessed with godly inspiration to discern cheese from chalk, the matters being so evidently discoursed by learned divines, and they have sway about the Prince, and would bring Her Majesty to the truth; but being deceived, I can only pray God to indue her and them with His grace to know and fear Him aright.

*Calendar of State Papers Domestic, Addenda, 1566–79*, vol. xxi, 56; C. Sharp, *Memorials of the Rebellion of 1569*, London, 1840, p. 189.

# BIBLIOGRAPHY

## PRIMARY SOURCES

### Chapters 1 and 2

Sir Thomas Smith's description of English society can be found in *De Republica Anglorum*, ed. by L. Alston, Cambridge, 1906 (reprinted Irish University Press, 1972) pp. 31–47. The attitude of Tudor governments to rebellion can best be studied through the more important propaganda works of 1536, 1549 and 1570. Among these are: Richard Morison, *A Remedy for sedition concerning the true and loyal obeysance that commons owe unto their prince*, Berthelet, 1536; Richard Morison, *A Lamentation in which is shewed what ruin cometh of seditious rebellion*, Berthelet, 1536; John Cheke, *The Hurt of Sedition how grievous it is to a commonwealth*, J. Daye & W. Seres, 1549; R.B. Bond (ed.), *Certain Sermons or Homilies (1547)* and *A Homily against Disobedience and Wilful Rebellion (1570)*, Toronto U.P., 1987.

The anthology in *English Historical Documents* provides a comprehensive survey of contemporary attitudes to social obligations and to rebellion [134].

### Chapter 3

The standard account of the Cornish Rising of 1497 is in 'The Anglica Historia of Polydore Vergil', ed. D. Hay, Camden Society, 3rd series, vol. lxxiv, 1950 [134 *p. 133*]. Later accounts, such as Bacon's, were based on Vergil, who wrote not many years after the events he described, albeit from a London-based and official viewpoint. The London Chronicle, which is in the Cotton manuscripts in the British Library, Vitellius A xvi, is printed in C.L. Kingsford, *Chronicles of London*, Clarendon Press, 1905. New material is presented in I. Arthurson [2].

Edward Hall's Chronicle provides the most useful account of the Amicable Grant. A number of the reports to Wolsey from the provinces are printed in the *Letters and Papers of Henry VIII*, vol. iv (1). New East Anglian material is used in the studies by G. Bernard, D. MacCulloch, R. Woods Jr. [13; 86; 138].

### Chapter 4

The main body of documentary material on the Pilgrimage of Grace is conveniently assembled in the *Letters and Papers of Henry VIII*, vols xi and xii (1). In 1890 M. Bateson printed important documents relating to Robert Aske's examination [3].

A comprehensive and indispensable account of the Pilgrimage was published by M.H. and R. Dodds in 1915 [44]. It is based on a careful analysis of the State Paper material. A valuable supplementary source from Bodleian Library, MS Jesus 74 consists of summaries of State Papers now lost, made in the early seventeenth century by Lord Herbert of Chirbury's secretary, Thomas Master: it has been published by Richard Hoyle [61]. Another interesting new discovery, a poem by William Calverley, is announced by J. Liedl [78].

## Chapter 5

The only full contemporary description of the Western Rebellion is by John Hooker, who was an eye-witness of the siege of Exeter. It is detailed and vividly written. There are several versions of it, the most available being that in Hooker's *Description of the City of Exeter*, published by the Devon and Cornwall Record Society in two volumes in 1919 (Preface and Index 1947). Hooker was twenty-four in 1549. He was educated at the school kept by Dr John Moreman, the Vicar of Menheniot [*Doc. 12, article 11*] and then at Oxford. He was converted to Protestantism when visiting Strasbourg where he met Peter Martyr and his bias is evident in his narrative.

Nicholas Pocock's 'Troubles connected with the Prayer Book of 1549', Camden Society, new series, vol. xxxvii, 1884, is a useful collection of sources. Somerset's reply to the rebels can be found in Foxe's *Acts and Monuments*, vol. v, and Cranmer's in his *Works*, Parker Society edn, vol. ii.

Julian Cornwall [30] makes use of muster returns and Exchequer papers to elucidate the military scene, and of lay subsidy rolls for the social and economic background. The previous standard account [109], which was published in 1913, is still worth consulting for it prints a number of important sources. Joyce Youings [140] suggests new directions of inquiry in original sources.

## Chapter 6

The most important source is Nicholas Sotherton's narrative, 'The Commoyson in Norfolk, 1549', available in print [7]. The sole manuscript copy is in the British Library. It is impossible to be certain which of two or more Nicholas Sothertons living in Norwich in the mid-sixteenth century wrote the account: very likely the Nicholas Sotherton whose father was mayor of Norwich in 1539. The account was probably written a few years after 1549: although it is extremely vivid, Sotherton makes it clear that he did not witness the events.

In 1575 Alexander Neville, one of the younger secretaries of Archbishop Parker, was the first to publish an account of the rebellion, *De Furoribus Norfolciensium Ketto Duce*. Parker was the son of a Norwich worsted weaver and lived his early life in East Anglia. He visited the rebels' camp in 1549 and the ecclesiastical historian John Strype maintained in his *Life* of the Archbishop, published in 1711, that 'he supplied the author with many instructions and remarks, while he was writing, being himself so well acquainted with the subject'. For remarks about the bias displayed by both Sotherton and Neville against the rebels see D. MacCulloch in [31]. A statement of the case for the commons and a perceptive analysis of 'covetousness' as the cause of the rebellion, in Hugh Latimer's last sermon before Edward VI, is printed in *English Historical Documents* [134 *pp. 354–6*].

Studies by D. MacCulloch [84; 31; 86 *Part IV*] draw on new sources; the account written in the last century, although difficult to obtain, is also still useful [112]. Judicial records have been used to throw light on the local economic factors which caused the rebellion [15; 56; 98].

## Chapter 7

The only detailed contemporary account of Wyatt's Rebellion is by John Proctor, a Tonbridge schoolmaster, who in his patriotic treatise *The Historie of Wyate's Rebellion* intended, by showing that it was a heretical movement, to present 'the lamentable image of hateful Rebellion for the increase of obedience'. Proctor's work is reprinted by E. Arber in *An English Garner*, London, 1877–96, vol. viii, and by A.F. Pollard in *Tudor Tracts, 1532–1588*, Westminster, 1903. There are shorter accounts of the rebellion in the 'Greyfriars Chronicle', Camden Society, first series, vol. liii, 1852, the 'Tower Chronicle', Camden Society, first series, vol. xlviii, 1850, and in Holinshed's Chronicles.

## Chapter 8

A large proportion of the state papers relating to the Northern Rebellion are in print and can be found in State Papers Domestic, Addenda, 1566–79, *Sir Ralph Sadler's State Papers and Letters*, ed. A. Clifford, Edinburgh, 1809, important manuscript sources, such as Humberston's survey of the estates of the attainted earls (1570), in the Public Record Office. In 1840 Sir Cuthbert Sharp printed documents from the Bowes Manuscripts, which contain many of Sir George Bowes's letters written during the rebellion, his memorandum on the rebellion and the rebel proclamation. In 1846 J. Raine printed depositions made in the court of Durham respecting the rebellion, in the Surtees Society, vol. xxi. In 1887 H.B. McCall printed and analysed the material in the Bowes papers concerned with the executions following the rebellion [90].

## Chapter 9

The quotation from Lord Thomas Seymour in 1549 is taken from Public Record Office, SP10/6/7, f.19r (*Calendar of State Papers Domestic, Edward VI*, no. 182; 112 *p. 15*).

SECONDARY SOURCES

1    Alsop, J.D., 'Latimer, the Commonwealth of Kent and the 1549 rebellions', *Historical Journal*, 28, 1985.
2    Arthurson, I., 'The rising of 1497: a revolt of the peasantry', in *People, Politics and Community in the Later Middle Ages*, ed. J. Rosenthal and C. Richmond, Alan Sutton, 1987.
3    Bateson, M., 'The Pilgrimage of Grace and Aske's examination', *English Historical Review*, 1890.
4    Bean, J.M.W., *The Estates of the Percy Family 1461–1537*, Oxford U.P., 1958.
5    Bean, J.M.W., *The Decline of English Feudalism*, Manchester U.P., 1968.
6    Beer, B.L., 'London and the Rebellion of 1548–1549', *Journal of British Studies*, 12, 1972.
7    Beer, B.L., ' "The Commoyson in Norfolk, 1549": a narrative of popular rebellion in sixteenth-century England', *Journal of Medieval and Renaissance Studies*, 6, 1976.
8    Beer, B.L., *Rebellion and Riot: Popular Disorder in England during the Reign of Edward VI*, Kent State U.P., 1982.
9    Beer, B.L., 'John Stow and Tudor rebellions 1549–1569', *Journal of British Studies*, 27, 1988.
10   Bennett, M.J., 'Henry VII and the Northern Rising of 1489', *English Historical Review*, 105, 1990.
11   Bercé, Y.-M., tr. J. Bergin, *Revolt and Revolution in Early Modern Europe: An Essay on the History of Political Violence*, Manchester U.P., 1987.
12   Beresford, M.W., *The Lost Villages of England*, Lutterworth, 1954.
13   Bernard, G.W., *War, Taxation and Rebellion in Early Tudor England*, Harvester, 1986.
14   Bernard, G.W. and Hoyle, R.W., 'The instructions for the levying of the Amicable Grant, March 1525', *Historical Research*, 67, 1994.
15   Bindoff, S.T., *Kett's Rebellion*, Historical Association, 1949.
16   Bossy, J., 'The character of Elizabethan Catholicism', *Past and Present*, 21, 1962.
17   Boynton, L., *The Elizabethan Militia*, Routledge & Kegan Paul, 1967.
18   Brooks, F.W., *The Council of the North*, Historical Association, 1953.
19   Bush, M.L., *The Government Policy of Protector Somerset*, Edward Arnold, 1975.
20   Bush, M.L., ' "Enhancements and importunate charges": an analysis of the tax complaints of October 1536', *Albion*, 22, 1990.
21   Bush, M.L., ' "Up for the Commonweal": the significance of tax grievances in the English rebellions of 1536', *English Historical Review*, 106, 1991.
22   Bush, M.L., 'Tax reform and rebellion in early Tudor England', *History*, 76, 1991.

23  Bush, M.L., 'Captain Poverty and the Pilgrimage of Grace', *Historical Research*, 156, 1992.

24  Bush, M.L., 'Tenant right under the Tudors: a revision revised', *Bulletin of the John Rylands Library*, 77, 1995.

25  Bush, M.L., *The Pilgrimage of Grace: A Study of the Rebel Armies of October 1536*, Manchester U.P., 1996.

26  Clark, P., 'Popular protest and disturbance in Kent, 1558–1640', *Economic History Review*, 29, 1976.

27  Clark, P., *English Provincial Society from the Reformation to the Revolution*, Harvester, 1977.

28  Clark, P., ed., *The European Crisis of the 1590s*, George Allen & Unwin, 1985.

29  Collinson, P., *The Elizabethan Puritan Movement*, Cape, 1967.

30  Cornwall, J., *Revolt of the Peasantry*, Routledge & Kegan Paul, 1977.

31  Cornwall, J., 'Kett's Rebellion: a comment', *Past and Present*, 93, 1981, and MacCulloch, D., 'Kett's Rebellion: a reply', *Past and Present*, 93, 1981, repr. in [117].

32  Cressy, D., *Literacy and the Social Order*, Cambridge U.P., 1980.

33  Cross, C., *The Puritan Earl*, Macmillan, 1966.

34  Cross, C., Loades, D. and Scarisbrick, J.J., eds, *Law and Government under the Tudors*, Cambridge U.P., 1987.

35  Davies, C.S.L., 'The Pilgrimage of Grace reconsidered', *Past and Present*, 41, 1968.

36  Davies, C.S.L., 'Popular religion and the Pilgrimage of Grace', in [50].

37  Dickens, A.G., *Lollards and Protestants in the Diocese of York*, Oxford U.P., 1959.

38  Dickens, A.G., *Thomas Cromwell and the English Reformation*, English Universities Press, 1959.

39  Dickens, A.G., *The English Reformation*, Batsford, 1964.

40  Dickens, A.G., 'Sedition and conspiracy in Yorkshire during the later years of Henry VIII', *Yorkshire Archaeological Journal*, 34, 1939. Repr. in Dickens, A.G., *Reformation Studies*, Hambledon Press, 1982.

41  Dickens, A.G., 'Some popular reactions to the Edwardian Reformation in Yorkshire', *Yorkshire Archaeological Journal*, 34, 1939. Repr. in Dickens, *Reformation Studies*.

42  Dickens, A.G., 'The first stages of Romanist recusancy in Yorkshire', *Yorkshire Archaeological Journal*, 35, 1941. Repr. in Dickens, *Reformation Studies*.

43  Dickens, A.G., 'Secular and religious motivation in the Pilgrimage of Grace', in *Studies in Church History*, ed. G.J. Cuming, vol. 4, 1967.

44  Dodds, M.H. and Dodds, R., *The Pilgrimage of Grace and the Exeter Conspiracy*, Cambridge U.P., 1915.

45  Ellis, S.G., 'Henry VIII, rebellion and the rule of law', *Historical Journal*, 24, 1981.

46  Elton, G.R., *Policy and Police*, Cambridge U.P., 1972.

47  Elton, G.R., *Reform and Reformation*, Edward Arnold, 1977.

48   Elton, G.R., 'Politics and the Pilgrimage of Grace', in Elton, *Studies in Tudor and Stuart Politics and Government*, vol. 3, 4 vols, Cambridge U.P., 1974–92. Repr. from *After the Reformation*, ed. B. Malament, Yale U.P., 1980.

49   Elton, G.R., *The Tudor Constitution*, revised edn, Cambridge U.P., 1982.

50   Fletcher, A. and Stevenson, J., eds, *Order and Disorder in Early Modern England*, Cambridge U.P., 1985.

51   Fox, A., 'Prophecies and politics in the reign of Henry VIII', in Fox, A. and Guy, J., *Reassessing the Henrician Age*, Basil Blackwell, 1986.

52   Gunn, S.J., 'Peers, commons and gentry in the Lincolnshire Revolt of 1536', *Past and Present*, 123, May 1989.

53   Guy, J., ed., *The Reign of Elizabeth I: Court and Culture in the Last Decade*, Cambridge U.P., 1995.

54   Hacket, H., *Virgin Mother, Maiden Queen: Elizabeth I and the Cult of the Virgin Mary*, Macmillan, 1995.

55   Haigh, C., *The Last Days of the Lancashire Monasteries and the Pilgrimage of Grace*, Chetham Society, 17, 1969.

56   Hammond, R.J., 'The social and economic circumstances of Kett's Rebellion', PhD thesis, University of London, 1934.

57   Harrison, S.M., *The Pilgrimage of Grace in the Lake Counties, 1536–7*, Royal Historical Society, 1981.

58   Hicks, M.A., 'The Yorkshire rebellion of 1489 reconsidered', *Northern History*, 22, 1986.

59   Hill, C., 'The many-headed monster in Tudor and Stuart England', in *From the Renaissance to the Counter-Reformation*, ed. C.H. Carter, Cape, 1966.

60   Hoskins, W.J., 'Harvest fluctuations and English economic history 1480–1619', *Agricultural History Review*, 12, part I, 1964.

61   Hoyle, R.W., 'Thomas Master's narrative of the Pilgrimage of Grace', *Northern History*, 21, 1985.

62   Hoyle, R.W., 'The 1st Earl of Cumberland: a reputation reassessed', *Northern History*, 22, 1986.

63   Hoyle, R.W., 'Crown, parliament and taxation in sixteenth-century England', *English Historical Review*, 109, 1994.

64   Ives, E.W., 'The genesis of the Statute of Uses', *English Historical Review*, 82, 1967.

65   James, M.E., *Change and Continuity in the Tudor North*, Borthwick Papers, 27, St Anthony's Press, York, 1965. Repr. in James, M.E., *Society, Politics and Culture: Studies in Early Modern England*, Cambridge U.P., 1986.

66   James, M.E., *A Tudor Magnate and the Tudor State*, Borthwick Papers, 30, St Anthony's Press, York, 1966. Repr. in James, *Society, Politics and Culture*.

67   James, M.E., 'The First Earl of Cumberland (1493–1542) and the decline of northern feudalism', *Northern History*, 1, 1966. Repr. in James, *Society, Politics and Culture*.

68  James, M.E., 'Obedience and dissent in Henrician England: the Lincolnshire Rebellion 1536', *Past and Present*, 48, 1970. Repr. in James, *Society, Politics and Culture*.

69  James, M.E., 'The concept of order and the Northern Rising', *Past and Present*, 60, 1973. Repr. in James, *Society, Politics and Culture*.

70  James, M.E., *Family, Lineage and Civil Society*, Oxford U.P., 1974.

71  Janson, S.L., *Political Protest and Prophecy under Henry VIII*, Cambridge U.P., 1991.

72  Jones, W.P.D., *The Tudor Commonwealth*, Athlone Press, 1970.

73  Jordan, W.K., *Edward VI: The Young King*, Allen & Unwin, 1968.

74  Jordan, W.K., *Edward VI: The Threshold of Power*, Allen & Unwin, 1970.

75  Kerridge, E., 'The movement of rent 1540–1640', *Economic History Review*, 6, 1953. Repr. in *Essays in Economic History*, vol. 2, ed. E.M. Carus-Wilson, 3 vols, Edward Arnold, 1962.

76  Knowles, D., *The Religious Orders in England*, vol. 3, 3 vols, Cambridge U.P., 1961.

77  Land, S.K., *Kett's Rebellion: The Norfolk Rising of 1549*, Boydell, 1977.

78  Liedl, J., 'The penitent Pilgrim: William Calverley and the Pilgrimage of Grace', *Sixteenth Century Journal*, 25, 1994.

79  Lindley, K., 'Riot prevention and control in early Stuart London', *Transactions of the Royal Historical Society*, 5th series, 33, 1983.

80  Loades, D.M., *Two Tudor Conspiracies*, Cambridge U.P., 1965.

81  Loades, D.M., *The Papers of George Wyatt*, Camden Society, 4th series, 5, 1968.

82  MacCaffrey, W., *The Shaping of the Elizabethan Regime*, Cape, 1969.

83  MacCaffrey, W., *Elizabeth I: War and Politics*, Princeton U.P., 1992.

84  MacCulloch, D., 'Kett's Rebellion in Context', *Past and Present*, 84, 1979, reprinted in [117].

85  MacCulloch, D., 'The "Vita Mariae Angliae Reginae" of Robert Wingfield of Brantham', *Camden Miscellany* 28, Camden Society, 4th series, 29, 1984.

86  MacCulloch, D., *Suffolk and the Tudors: Politics and Religion in an English County 1500–1600*, Oxford U.P., 1986.

87  MacCulloch, D., ed., *The Reign of Henry VIII: Politics, Policy and Piety*, Macmillan, 1995.

88  MacCulloch, D., *Thomas Cranmer: A Life*, Yale U.P., 1996.

89  McConica, J.K., *English Humanists and Reformation Politics*, Oxford U.P., 1965.

90  McCall, H.B., 'Executions after the Northern Rebellion', *Yorkshire Archaeological Journal*, 18, 1887.

91  Manning, R.B., 'Violence and social conflict in mid-Tudor rebellions', *Journal of British Studies*, 16, 1977.

92  Manning, R.B., 'The origins of the doctrine of sedition', *Albion*, 12, 1980.

93  Manning, R.B., *Village Revolts. Social Protest and Popular Disturbances in England 1509–1640*, Oxford U.P., 1987.

94  Marcombe, D., 'A rude and heady people: the local community and

the rebellion of the northern Earls', in *The Last Principality. Religion and Society in the Bishopric of Durham, 1494–1660*, ed. D. Marcombe, University of Nottingham, 1987.

95  Menmuir, C., *The Rebellion of the Earls of Northumberland and Westmorland*, 1569, Newcastle, 1907.

96  Moreton, C.E., 'The Walsingham conspiracy of 1537', *Historical Research*, 63, 1990.

97  Moreton, C.E., *The Townshends and Their World*, Oxford U.P., 1992.

98  Moreton, C.E., 'Mid-Tudor trespass: a break-in at Norwich, 1549', *English Historical Review*, 108, 1993.

99  Morgan, H., *Tyrone's Rebellion: The Outbreak of the Nine Years War in Tudor Ireland*, Boydell, 1993.

100  Neale, J.E., *Queen Elizabeth*, Cape, 1934.

101  Neale, J.E., *Elizabeth I and her Parliaments*, 2 vols, Cape, 1953.

102  Palliser, D.M., *Tudor York*, Oxford U.P., 1979.

103  Phelps Brown, E.H. and Hopkins, S.U., 'Seven centuries of the prices of consumables compared with builders' wage rates', *Economica*, 1956. Repr. in *Essays in Economic History*, vol. 2, ed. E.M. Carus-Wilson, 3 vols, Edward Arnold, 1962.

104  Phythian-Adams, C., *Desolation of a City*, Cambridge U.P., 1979.

105  Pollitt, R., 'The defeat of the northern rebellion and the shaping of Anglo-Scottish relations', *Scottish Historical Review*, 64, 1985.

106  Pound, J.F., 'The social and trade structure of Norwich 1525–75', *Past and Present*, 34, 1966.

107  Reid, R.R., 'The rebellion of the Northern Earls', *Transactions of the Royal Historical Society*, first series, 20, 1906.

108  Reid, R.R., *The King's Council of the North*, Longman, 1921.

109  Rose-Troup, F., *The Western Rebellion of 1549*, Smith, Elder, 1913.

110  Rowse, A.L., *Tudor Cornwall*, Cape, 1951.

111  Russell, C.S.R., 'Arguments for religious unity in England 1530–1650', *Journal of Ecclesiastical History*, 18, 1967.

112  Russell, F.W., *Kett's Rebellion in Norfolk*, Longman, 1859.

113  Scarisbrick, J.J., *Henry VIII*, Eyre & Spottiswode, 1968.

114  Schofield, R., 'Parliamentary lay taxation 1485–1547', PhD thesis, Cambridge University, 1963.

115  Schofield, R., 'Taxation and the political limits of the Tudor state', in [34].

116  Simpson, A., *The Wealth of the Gentry*, Cambridge U.P., 1963.

117  Slack, P., ed., *Rebellion, Popular Protest and the Social Order in Early Modern England*, Cambridge U.P., 1984.

118  Smith, R.B., *Land and Politics in the England of Henry VIII*, Oxford U.P., 1970.

119  Stone, L., *The Crisis of the Aristocracy*, Oxford U.P., 1965.

120  Stone, L., 'Social mobility in England 1500–1700', *Past and Present*, 33, 1966.

121  Stoyle, M., ' "Pagans or paragons?" Images of the Cornish during the English Civil War', *English Historical Review*, 111, 1996.

122 Tawney, R.H., *The Agrarian Problem in the Sixteenth Century*, Longman, 1912.
123 Tawney, R.H. and Power, E., eds, *Tudor Economic Documents*, vol. 3, 3 vols, Longman, 1924.
124 Taylor, S.E., 'The crown and the north of England 1559–1570', PhD thesis, Manchester University, 1981.
125 Thirsk, J., ed., *The Agrarian History of England*, vol. 4, 8 vols, Cambridge U.P., 1967.
126 Thomas, K.V., *Religion and the Decline of Magic*, Weidenfeld & Nicolson, 1971.
127 Thompson, J.A.F., *The Later Lollards*, Oxford U.P., 1965.
128 Thorp, M., 'Religion and the Wyatt Rebellion of 1554', *Church History*, 48, 1979.
129 Tillyard, E.M.W., *The Elizabethan World Picture*, Chatto & Windus 1943 (reprinted by Penguin, 1963).
130 Tyler, P., 'The significance of the ecclesiastical commission at York', *Northern History*, 2, 1967.
131 Underdown, D., *Revel, Riot and Rebellion: Popular Politics and Culture in England 1603–1660*, Oxford U.P., 1985.
132 Walter, J., 'A "Rising of the People"? The Oxfordshire rising of 1596', *Past and Present*, 107, May 1985.
133 Willen, D., 'Lord Russell and the western counties 1539–1555', *Journal of British Studies*, 15, 1975.
134 Williams, C.H., *English Historical Documents, v, 1485–1558*, Eyre & Spottiswode, 1967.
135 Williams, N., *Thomas Howard, Fourth Duke of Norfolk*, Barrie & Rockcliff, 1964.
136 Williams, P., 'Rebellion and revolution in early modern England', in *War and Society: Essays in Honour of John Western*, ed. M.R.D. Foot, Manchester U.P., 1973.
137 Williams, P., *The Tudor Regime*, Oxford U.P., 1979.
138 Woods, R., 'Individuals in the rioting crowd: a new approach', *Journal of Interdisciplinary History*, 14, 1983.
139 Woodward, G.W.O., *The Dissolution of the Monasteries*, Blandford, 1966.
140 Youings, J., 'The South-Western Rebellion of 1549', *Southern History*, 1, 1979.
141 Zagorin, P., *Rebels and Rulers 1500–1660*, 2 vols, Cambridge U.P., 1982.
142 Zeeveld, W.G., *Foundations of Tudor Policy*, Harvard U.P., 1948.

# INDEX